Rodgers + Hammerstein's

CINDERELLA

The Applause Libretto Library Series

Rodgers + Hammerstein's

CINDERELLA

Music by Richard Rodgers
Lyrics by Oscar Hammerstein II
New Book by Douglas Carter Beane
Original Book by Oscar Hammerstein II

APPLAUSE
THEATRE & CINEMA BOOKS

Published in 2014 by applause Theatre & Cinema Books
an Imprint of Globe Pequot, the trade division of
The Rowman & Littlefield Publishing Group, Inc.
4501 Forbes Boulevard, Suite 200
Lanham, Maryland 20706

Distributed by NATIONAL BOOK NETWORK

Photograph credits can be found on page 145, which constitutes an extension of this copyright page.
Book compositor: Mark Lerner

Library of Congress Cataloging-in-Publication Data

Rodgers, Richard, 1902–1979.
[Cinderella. Libretto]
Cinderella : the complete book and lyrics of the Broadway musical / Music by Richard Rodgers ; lyrics by Oscar Hammerstein II ; new book by Douglas Carter Beane ; original book by Oscar Hammerstein.
    pages cm
Includes bibliographical references and index.
ISBN 978-1-4803-5555-2 (pbk. : alk. paper)
1. Musicals—Librettos. I. Hammerstein, Oscar, II, 1895–1960. II. Beane, Douglas Carter, 1959– III. Hammerstein, Oscar. IV. Title.
ML50.R67C5 2014
782.I'40268--dc23
                    2014031968

www.applausebooks.com

CONTENTS

FOREWORD

To the Matter of Kindness, Social Justice, and a Red Rambler

I am seated in the offices of Rodgers & Hammerstein in Manhattan, and let me assure you they look nothing as they ought. One would think they'd be woody and red carpety and cigarette smokey and cocktails at five-ish. They are actually in a glamorous, industrial chic downtown loft—the kind that used to house your great aunt Sadie making shirtfronts and now holds movie actors with big bucks. In the center of the staircase of this austere workspace and enclosed in glass are the Tonys and Oscars and Emmys and a Johnny Mop (Dorothy Rodgers invented it, did you know that? Now you do). I am waiting to meet Ted Chapin, the lord and master of all things Rodgers & Hammerstein. The surrey with the fringe on top, the lonely goatherd, the Bali Ha'i. I have been sent by Robyn Goodman, the commercial producer, to pitch my fresh new take on *Cinderella* to the folks at R & H so that we may have the rights to finally bring this show to Broadway for the first time. A less likely moment I cannot imagine.

As I am about to give myself a moment to contemplate my fresh new take, the late-afternoon sun splashes into my eyes from the large factory-sized window. I must have winced because quite quickly the receptionist apologizes—"Oh, let me pull down the shade." And when she does, there is a moment of magic. There, printed onto the shade, a large black-and-white photograph of Richard Rodgers and Oscar Hammerstein. They are both lighted from behind by the sun and from within with what we can only imagine is a new idea. And like that I am transported back to a time in my vaguely recalled youth.

I am in a red Rambler on an autumn Sunday afternoon drive with my family. And we are all singing Rodgers & Hammerstein scores, ticking off the songs one by one, just like the cast albums. This is before Sirius Broadway and fears of a hole in the ozone layer, so people go on pointless endless car drives and sing show tunes. Whole families at a time, and boy, are we happy. Rodgers & Hammerstein have a way of giving you a lift. They have a way of making you think the world can be a good place and that mankind and civilization will sort it out if we all will just be better.

So that is the image I have when I look at big Oscar's and big Richard's faces on the blinds. And I feel comfort, ease, strength even. "Climb ev'ry mountain, ford every stream." Done and done.

Ted Chapin slides into the lobby as effortlessly as Lady Thiang with the biggest, warmest smile, and in no time I am in an office with Richard Rodgers's actual chairs and piano, and I am telling him my fresh new take for *Cinderella*. Which maybe is not so fresh and new after all—maybe that's the freshest newest thing to do?

I suggest we use the story R & H used as their basis—the fable by Perrault. But I mean the actual fairy tale, not the improved version we Americans know. It will give us what Cinderella has always craved: motivation and (*yes!*) a second act. You see, in the original version Cinderella is kind in a world that has become entrenched in treachery and ridicule. That's what she brings to the court. It's why the Prince is attracted to her. She also meets the Prince not once but twice: first at a ball and then at a banquet. There is the power of kindness, turning a court used to bitterness into a joyful place again. There is a first act curtain that would keep people talking all through the intermission.

The gifts keep adding up. There is a sister who turns out to be a friend and helps Cinderella. And Sis has a boyfriend! We have a secondary comedy love couple quicker than you can say "Will and Ado Annie."

I also will be drawing from the exquisite work of R & H. The wonderful anachronistic lyrics of Oscar's, with his "Why would a fella" and in a world of swords, someone forgetting to "bring my gun." I'll do that in the dialogue. And there is the wonderful "A Lovely Night," which showed that this broken family was yearning to love one another and hope together. I will use the craftsmanship of "Driving Through the Moonlight" falling into "A Lovely Night" as a foundation on which to build a full-scale musical.

And finally I will use as an influence who Richard and Oscar were in their lives. Their work most always reflected the need for social justice and understanding. But also the actions of their lives in causes and movements.

And then as fast and rollicky as a red Rambler ride, I have the go-ahead to write a draft. I use the terrific *Complete Lyrics of Oscar Hammerstein II* to get some new songs to fill out the score. I'll see what works lyrically and pray Mr. Rodgers has a good tune. (He always does, but sometimes the lyrics don't even have a melody—they are abandoned too early.) From the process comes a wonderful opening chorus cut from *South Pacific,* which magically has the words "fairy tale book." "Me, Who Am I?" for the Prince—cut from an opening montage in *Me and Juliet.* A song, "He Was Tall," for Cinderella after the ball, cut from *The King and I.* "Now Is the Time," also cut from *South Pacific,* will be a great song for the sister's boyfriend. Oh, I'll make him a student protestor.

And soon wonderful people, all with killer ideas, jump in. David Chase, along with Bruce Pomahac, come up with bewitching discoveries that complement what I'm writing. Josh Rhodes, the choreographer, blends "Now Is the Time" and "The Prince Is Giving a Ball" in a way that is fun to watch but also says a little something about how we love to be distracted from our problems. Mark Brokaw weaves it all together. William Ivey Long, Anna Louizos, and Kenny Posner keep it spinning it into magic and keep it real.

And then I am backstage on opening night. It's curtain call and people are standing and yelling and generally going nuts. Not just because we did it, but because there is the unmistakable feeling that this is a Rodgers & Hammerstein premiere on Broadway. And I am ready to take my bow as author. Fancy me. And Robyn Goodman hands me a large photograph of Richard and Oscar to take with me.

But then I've been taking them with me all along. As far back as the red Rambler.

DCB

INTRODUCTION

In the mid-1950s, Rodgers and Hammerstein were the kings of Broadway. So it was logical that they would be the ones for CBS-TV to commission to create a new musical especially for television. NBC had success with *Peter Pan* starring Mary Martin, and CBS wanted to match that success. They had a deal for the services of Julie Andrews, then playing in *My Fair Lady* on Broadway, and the notion of creating a classic *Cinderella* to star Julie Andrews seemed like a natural fit. So in early September 1956, it was announced that in the following spring, a new Rodgers & Hammerstein musical would premiere—live—on CBS.

The entire CBS television version of *Cinderella* was written, cast, designed, built, arranged, orchestrated, and mounted seven months after the announcement, on Sunday, March 31, 1957. It was a 90-minute "live in color" (for the very few color television sets in the country) special, and it was seen by 107 million viewers, averaging 4.43 people per television set in the country! Clearly, it was a major cultural event.

Television has seen two more versions of the Rodgers & Hammerstein *Cinderella*. One was on CBS in 1965, starring Lesley Ann Warren, which was filmed on videotape so it could be re-broadcast over many years. And then, in 1997, a new version, with a multi-cultural cast starring Whitney Houston and Brandy, was made for ABC. Both were successful, and each one gathered a new generation of fans.

Interestingly, Oscar Hammerstein's teleplay for the original 1957 version became popular onstage. Professional theaters across the country found that their audiences were captivated by the score and story, and schools and community theaters enjoyed revisiting a favorite version of the age-old tale, with a bunch of tuneful Rodgers & Hammerstein songs.

Fast-forward to a trip I took to Israel in 2008, hosted by Broadway producer Manny Azenberg. Among the 20 intrepid New Yorkers who wandered over the Golan Heights and floated on the Dead Sea was Robyn Goodman, a producer whose acquaintance I had made but who I didn't really know that well. We enjoyed each other's company, and at some point she asked me whether there wasn't something we could work on together. Off the top of my head, without much thought, I said, "You know, no one has yet figured out how to make a Broadway-worthy version of the Rodgers & Hammerstein *Cinderella*." The wheels of her producer's mind started to turn, and we tossed notions around about what a Broadway *Cinderella* could be, who could help create the new world for the classic score to fit, and how to find a modern sensibility that would speak directly to audiences of today while honoring the best of what Rodgers & Hammerstein were all about.

Well, Douglas Carter Beane was her first choice to write it, and he came into the office to explore cut songs and less-well-known songs to augment the score. Director Mark Brokaw and choreographer Josh Rhodes came on board, as did the rather brilliant design team of Anna Louizos, Donald Holder, Kenneth Posner, Nevin Steinberg, and William Ivey Long. Musical supervisor David Chase and musical director Andy Einhorn rounded out the creative team, and together they succeeded more than I could have hoped.

So I give a nod of thanks to everyone who helped create this show. (And a summer '14 thanks to the invaluable Andrew Marco.)

Between these pages you have Rodgers + Hammerstein's *Cinderella*—that "+" being one modern way to brand this show. It is fun, it is classic, and it is entirely appropriate for our time.

Ted Chapin
The Rodgers & Hammerstein Organization

PUBLISHER'S NOTE

Rodgers + Hammerstein's

CINDERELLA

Rodgers + Hammerstein's Cinderella, *the first Broadway appearance of the Rodgers & Hammerstein version of* Cinderella, *opened on March 3, 2013, at the Broadway Theatre, New York City, with the following cast:*

(In order of appearance)

Ella .... Laura Osnes
Giant.. Peter Nelson
Topher .... Santino Fontana
Lord Pinkleton ....Phumzile Sojola
Sebastian .... Peter Bartlett
Marie ....Victoria Clark
Jean-Michel ....Greg Hildreth
Madame...Harriet Harris
Gabrielle ....Marla Mindelle
Charlotte ....Ann Harada
Fox .... Heidi Giberson (puppet); Andy Mills
Raccoon .... Laura Irion (puppet); Cody Williams
Footman... Andy Mills
Driver .... Cody Williams
Lady of Ridicule...................................Jill Abramovitz

Ensemble: Jill Abramovitz, Kristine Bendul, Heidi Giberson, Stephanie Gibson, Shonica Gooden, Kendal Hartse, Robert Hartwell, Laura Irion, Andy Jones, Andy Mills, Linda Mugleston, Peter Nelson, Nick Spangler, Cody Williams, Branch Woodman, Kevin Worley

Produced by Robyn Goodman, Jill Furman, Stephen Kocis
Directed by Mark Brokaw
Choreographed by Josh Rhodes
Musical Adaptation, Supervision, and Arrangements by David Chase
Orchestrations by Danny Troob
Scenic Design by Anna Louizos
Costume Design by William Ivey Long
Lighting Design by Kenneth Posner
Sound Design by Nevin Steinberg
Hair and Wig Design by Paul Huntley
Music Direction and Conductor: Andy Einhorn
Production Stage Manager: Ira Mont
Associate Director: Gina Rattan
Associate Choreographer: Lee Wilkins
Press Representative: Sam Rudy Media Relations
Company Manager: Brig Berney
General Management: Richards/Climan, Inc.

Additional producer credits:
Edward Walson, Venetian Glass Productions, The Araca Group,
Luigi Caiola & Rose Caiola, Roy Furman, Walt Grossman,
Peter May/Sanford Robertson, Glass Slipper Productions
LLC/Eric Schmidt, Ted Liebowitz/James Spry, Blanket Fort
Productions
In association with Center Theatre Group and Charles Salameno

Produced by Arrangement with Rodgers & Hammerstein: An
Imagem Company

SCENES

Act One

Prologue: A Forest
Scene 1: A Rocky Glen
Scene 2: Outside Madame's Cottage
Scene 3: The Throne Room of the Royal Palace
Scene 4: The Town Square
Scene 5: Inside Madame's Cottage
Scene 6: Outside Madame's Cottage
Scene 7: Flight to the Castle
Scene 8: The Castle Ballroom
Scene 9: The Palace Steps

Act Two

Scene 1: The Palace Steps
Scene 2: The Forest
Scene 3: Outside, then Inside, Madame's Cottage
Scene 4: Another Part of the Forest
Scene 5: Inside Madame's Cottage
Scene 6: The Palace Steps
Scene 7: The Palace
Scene 8: The Royal Gardens

ACT ONE

Prologue

SCENE: *A Forest*
(ELLA, *a young, beautiful girl, in provincial clothes, enters with a cart, looking for firewood. We hear an unseen* CHORUS *sing.*)

CHORUS

The fields are aglow in autumn yellow,
And the sky is a robin's egg blue.
It makes you wish,
When you fall asleep,
You will dream about the view.
Bizarre and improbable and pretty
As a page from the fairy-tale books,
It makes you wish
That the world could be
As lovely as it looks.

ELLA

It makes you wish
That the world could be

ELLA & CHORUS

As lovely as it looks.

MADAME
(*Offstage*)

Cinderella!
(ELLA *runs off into the woods.*)

Scene One

SCENE: *A Rocky Glen*
(KNIGHTS *of the Royal Court stalk through the forest. Suddenly, a* GIANT *appears. The* KNIGHTS *and* GIANT *do battle. The towering* GIANT *quickly takes the upper hand, throwing* KNIGHTS *left and right.* TOPHER, *the Prince of the kingdom, appears in full battle splendor.* TOPHER *quickly outwits the* GIANT, *causing it to fall slowly to the ground.* TOPHER *takes a triumphant pose atop the* GIANT.)

TOPHER
I just wish I was doing something more important with my life.
(*A general groan of dismay from the soldiers—not this again.* SEBASTIAN, *the Lord Protector, an overly elegantly dressed man of the court, steps forward.* LORD PINKLETON *follows him.*)

SEBASTIAN
Worrying about that self-worth again, Prince Topher?

TOPHER
It all just comes too easily.

SEBASTIAN
The fact remains, sire—You will be king and very soon. When your sainted mother and father passed away and left you in my charge, I promised them when you came of age you would be prepared for your reign.
(*A* PAGE BOY *brings out the* PRINCE's *horse.*)

TOPHER
I know, Sebastian, I know. And I guess I am ready to be a king.

The thing of it is: I just don't even know who I am yet.

SEBASTIAN

I'm sure it will come to you. Until then, might I suggest faking it?

TOPHER

Really?

SEBASTIAN

You wouldn't be the first and you wouldn't be the last.

LORD PINKLETON

To the castle?

TOPHER

To the castle.
(TOPHER *mounts the horse.* SEBASTIAN *walks along as* TOPHER *rides on horseback.* PAGE BOYS *with banners and the* KNIGHTS *march with them. The scenery changes behind them.*)

TOPHER

Still. These questions. Nag me. Nag. Nag.
(*The horse whinnies.* TOPHER *pats the horse's neck as he rides*)
No, not you, Buttercup. I just wonder.
(*Sings*)
Me, who am I?
A far-from-perfect guy—
A bum who wants to do what's right
But often does what's wrong,
A kid whose voice is way off-key
But loves to sing a song,
A guy who dreams like a lion

But wakes up like a lamb—
Me, who am I
But the guy
I am?
That's
Who'm I.

KNIGHTS, SEBASTIAN, PINKLETON
His Royal Highness
Christopher Rupert—
Slayer of dragons—
Pitiless to ogres—
Destroyer of griffins and giants—
No friend to gargoyles!
(*The dragon flies overhead.*)

LORD PINKLETON
Dragon!

TOPHER
No, n-n-no, I got it! I got it! C'mon!

KNIGHTS, SEBASTIAN, PINKLETON
Nice to the needy—
Sportsman and poet—
A guy who dreams like a lion
But wakes up like a lamb—
(*The dragon shoots a giant fireball.* TOPHER *fires his slingshot.*
We hear the dragon fall and land with a massive "THUMP."
TOPHER *and the* KNIGHTS *react to the aftershock.*)

TOPHER

Me, who am I
But the guy I am?

KNIGHTS, SEBASTIAN, LORD PINKLETON

He's our hero!

TOPHER

Oh, stop.

KNIGHTS, SEBASTIAN, LORD PINKLETON

Such perfection!

TOPHER

That's very kind of you.

KNIGHTS, SEBASTIAN, PINKLETON

He's the kind of guy who we'd all like to be.

TOPHER

I appreciate it.

KNIGHTS, SEBASTIAN, PINKLETON

What's the use of
Self reflection?

TOPHER

Too much.

KNIGHTS, SEBASTIAN, PINKLETON

Church bells will ring
When you are king.

People will sing
There is no one quite like—

TOPHER	KNIGHTS
Me,	His Royal Highness
Who am I?	Christopher Rupert—
A far-from-perfect	Slayer of dragons—
Guy—	Pitiless to ogres—
A jerk who wants to do what's	Destroyer of griffins and
right	giants—
But often does what's wrong,	No friend to gargoyles!
A drip whose voice is way	Nice to the needy—
off-key	
But loves to sing a song,	Sportsman and poet—
A guy who dreams like a lion	Swordsman—Statesman—
But wakes up like a lamb—	Nifty dancer, sailor of the
	oceans
Me, who am I	Surveyor of the mountains
	and valleys
But the guy I am?	He's a prince
That's who'm	What a guy! What a guy!
I.	What a guy! What a guy!
That's	He's a plain and simple
Who'm	Complicated, fascinating
I.	Guy!
	What a guy!
Ha!	Guy!

(*The march ends outside* MADAME'*s cottage. The* KNIGHTS *march off.*)

Scene Two

SCENE: *Outside Madame's Cottage*
(*A provincial cottage, with a wishing well nearby. As* TOPHER
and his MEN *stop, a pumpkin rolls onstage, followed by* ELLA.
SEBASTIAN *stops the pumpkin with his foot.*)

SEBASTIAN

You there! Impoverished person! Fetch us some water!

ELLA

Yes, sir.

TOPHER

Don't talk to her that way. How do you know she's poor?

SEBASTIAN

Look at her. She's filthy.
(ELLA *draws water from the well into a gourd, which she then
gives to* TOPHER.)

ELLA

Here you are, sire.

TOPHER

Thank you, young lady. (*Seeing her and smiling*) That's very kind
of you.
(TOPHER *takes a sip of water and looks at* ELLA.)

ELLA
(*Blushing*)

It's just water.

SEBASTIAN

Give her some money.

TOPHER

Really?
(ELLA *exits with the pumpkin.*)

SEBASTIAN

Yes! It's charity! You have things and she doesn't. You're going to giver her some of your things, so she doesn't have a revolution and take all of your things.
(MARIE, *a woman in rags, enters.* ELLA *reenters with her cart.*)

MARIE

Spare change, any spare change?

SEBASTIAN

The moment charity is mentioned, out comes every lay-about!

TOPHER
(*Handing* MARIE *a coin*)
Here you are, old woman.

MARIE

Thank you. Bless you, kind sir.
(MARIE *reaches out to* TOPHER. SEBASTIAN *and* LORD PINKLE-TON *draw their swords.*)

SEBASTIAN

Be careful, my Lord, many of the very poor have weapons.

LORD PINKLETON

Be gone with you.

ELLA

No! Good sirs, that is merely Crazy Marie. She lives in the woods and comes to town only to gather what others throw away. She is gentle in every way. Sweet and delicate, but nuts.

TOPHER

She is harmless, I can tell. Sebastian, Lord Pinkleton, sheathe your swords. (*To* ELLA) You are a good friend to Marie. How lucky she is to have a true friend such as you. I wish I had a true friend.

SEBASTIAN

I'm standing right here.

LORD PINKLETON

Shall we journey on?

TOPHER

Very well, Pinkleton. (*Giving* ELLA *a coin*) Be well, young lady.

ELLA

I don't want charity.

TOPHER

Take the coin then as a present, in admiration for a true friend in this world. Buttercup! (TOPHER *begins to ride off, with his* FOL-LOWERS. *He remembers he has the drinking gourd*) Oh, here, sorry. (*Gives it back to* ELLA) Lot on my mind. (*Exits.*)

MARIE

Thank you for saving my life, dear Ella. I shall return the favor.

ELLA

I didn't do it to have a favor returned.
(ELLA *looks off in* TOPHER'*s direction.*)

MARIE

I have a shawl here that only has a few holes and smells of cabbage. You can wear it.

ELLA

Not necessary. What a handsome man that was, and so kind and generous.

MARIE

That is but not a man, that is Prince Topher, the slayer of giants and dragons. He has just returned to us from university. He is to be crowned king.

ELLA

That man? A world leader? But he appears to have a heart, mind, and soul, it can't be. Marie, you're crazy.

MARIE

Yes, I am. But that does not change the fact that he is our own Prince Topher and he has returned to be our ruler—look at your coin, dear.

ELLA
(*Looking at the coin*)

Why, it is him. From the left. Such silly ears. And the crown doesn't help things, he should wear a floppy hat. (*They laugh warmly*) Here Marie, please take this coin. Buy yourself something warm to eat.

(*As she hands the coin to* MARIE, JEAN-MICHEL, *a wild-haired, bespectacled revolutionary, enters.*)

JEAN-MICHEL

Why is it always the very poorest who are the most generous? It breaks my heart.

MARIE

Here is our Jean-Michel. He will spout gibberish now and bore us.

ELLA
(*To* MARIE)
Be nice. (*To* JEAN-MICHEL) Good day, Jean-Michel.

JEAN-MICHEL

And do you know why the poor are the kindest, Ella and Crazy Marie?

MARIE

No, but I have a feeling you are about to be most forthcoming.

JEAN-MICHEL

Because it is a corrupt system, with a smashed moral compass.

MARIE

You will forgive me if I just stagger about and mutter. (*She does so.*)

JEAN-MICHEL

Today I will be going alone to the castle to protest the corruption that riddles our government! You must come with me!

                            MADAME
                           (*Offstage*)
Cinderella!

                             MARIE
That is Madame, Ella's stepmother!

                         JEAN-MICHEL
I shall shout to the prince! He will have no choice but to listen!

                            MADAME
                           (*Offstage*)
Cinderella!

                             MARIE
You are in harm's way!

                         JEAN-MICHEL
I have a vision for what this kingdom could be.

                            MADAME
                           (*Entering*)
Cinderella! Help me with my parcels this instant! Cinderella,
lazy step-daughter, help me with my package! (ELLA *scrambles to
do so*) Careful! Careful!! No one knows the extreme torture I am
subjected to. (*Notices* MARIE *and* JEAN-MICHEL) I'm ignoring that.
Charlotte, Gabrielle, come daughters, come!
        (GABRELLE *and* CHARLOTTE *enter, beautifully dressed.*)

                           GABRIELLE
We are here, Mama!

CHARLOTTE

We are exhausted being as beautiful as we look.

MADAME

Cinderella, idle girl, come help your stepsisters with their shrewd purchases. Into the house, daughters—the real ones.

(MADAME *enters the house with* CHARLOTTE.)

GABRIELLE

(*Helping* ELLA *collect her packages*)

Madame isn't always terrible. Sometimes she sleeps.

JEAN-MICHEL

Gabrielle. I have brought from university a book for you, with pictures of how people in other lands live. And how they govern. Norway, Italy, Japan . . .

GABRIELLE

I have mentioned my interest in these places only in passing. And you have brought a whole book. (*Blushing*) Quit it, you.

JEAN-MICHEL

And four days from now I would like to take you on a date. I'm organizing a soup kitchen. We need someone to stir. And ladle.

MADAME

(*Re-entering*)

Gabrielle! Do not talk to that man. We are teetering precariously between upper-middle class and lower-upper class. We cannot be seen talking with a revolutionary. Into this house at once.

(GABRIELLE *gives the book back to* JEAN-MICHEL *and runs into the house.* MADAME *follows her into the house.*)

JEAN-MICHEL
Why do I care? Why do I try? I'll never be good enough for her. I will take this book and burn it!

MARIE
Why not give the book to dear Ella?

ELLA
If it's quite all right, Jean-Michel, I would love to look at your book of how other countries live.

JEAN-MICHEL
(*Hands* ELLA *the book*)
Then here, Ella. Take it. I shall go my way alone and live my own life. I'm a loner! (*To* MARIE) You're coming with me, right?

MARIE
Of course.

JEAN-MICHEL
Good.
(MARIE *and* JEAN-MICHEL *exit.* ELLA *looks at the book.*)

ELLA
A book. It's been so long since I owned something, just me.
(MADAME *enters from the cottage.* ELLA *quickly hides the book.*)

MADAME
Cinderella? Get in there and clean the kitchen.

ELLA
(*Sweetly*)

I've just finished it.

MADAME

Then prepare the dinner.

ELLA
(*With a bit of pride*)

It's on the stove.

MADAME

Then the bed must—

ELLA

Beds are turned down and your bed clothing is all laid out.

MADAME

Well. Where'd you get that book?

ELLA

Jean-Michel just gave it to me.

MADAME

So nice that people just give you gifts. Still Daddy's little girl.
(*Notices a coat hanging by the door*) And what's this doing here?

ELLA

That's my father's coat.

MADAME

It's rags.

ELLA

It's all I have to remember him by.

MADAME
(*Rips the coat*)
It's rags now. Clean the porch with these rags.
(MADAME *throws the coat on the ground and exits.* ELLA *picks it up and hugs it. She then sits on a stool with her book.*)

ELLA

I'm as mild and as meek as a mouse;
When I hear a command I obey.
But I know of a spot in my house
Where no one can stand in my way.
In my own little corner,
In my own little chair,
I can be whatever I want to be.
On the wing of my fancy
I can fly anywhere
And the world will open its arms to me.
I'm a young Norwegian princess or a milkmaid,
I'm the greatest prima donna in Milan,
I'm an heiress who has always had her silk made
By her own flock of silkworms in Japan!
I'm a girl men go mad for,
Love's a game I can play
With a cool and confident kind of air,
Just as long as I stay
In my own little corner,
All alone
In my own
Little chair.

(*A* FOX *emerges from the wood box*)
I can be whatever I want to be.
I'm a thief in Calcutta,
I'm a queen in Peru,
I'm a mermaid dancing upon the sea.
(*A* RACCOON *emerges from within a nearby tree*)
I'm a huntress on an African safari—
(It's a dang'rous type of sport and yet it's fun.)
In the night I sally forth to seek my quarry,
And I find I forgot to bring my gun!
I am lost in the jungle
All alone and unarmed
When I meet a lioness in her lair!
Then I'm glad to be back
In my own little corner,
All alone
In my own
Little chair.
> (*The song proper ends.* ELLA *sings as she wanders into the woods.*)

ELLA

I can be whatever I want to be,
> (TOPHER *appears on his throne.*)

TOPHER

Just as long as I stay
In my own little corner,

ELLA

All alone

TOPHER

All alone

ELLA

In my own

TOPHER

In my own

ELLA & TOPHER

Little chair.

(ELLA *exits into the woods.*)

Scene Three

SCENE: *The Throne Room of the Royal Palace*
(SEBASTIAN, PINKLETON, *and other* POLITICAL FIGURES *join*
TOPHER *in his throne room.*)

LORD PINKLETON

Your Majesty,
Your Majesty,
A list of the lords entreating thee.

TOPHER

A list of the lords entreating me with what?

LORD PINKLETON

A hundred and five requests.

TOPHER

That seems a lot.

SEBASTIAN

I'll take this. (*To* TOPHER) Your Majestic Highness, in honor of
your upcoming coronation we proudly proclaim your kingdom
a land of plenty and bounty. May I have the imprimatur of your
ring on this other announcement?

TOPHER

Oh right, sorry. What's it for?
(TOPHER *stamps the papers with his ring.*)

SEBASTIAN

It's complicated. Do you really want me to go into it?

JEAN-MICHEL

(*Offstage, as if outside the palace*)
Prince Topher, listen!

TOPHER

What was that?

JEAN-MICHEL

You must take responsibility for your actions!

TOPHER

Who's that yelling from the other side of the moat?

JEAN-MICHEL

The people are being treated unfairly by your government!

TOPHER

He seems upset.

SEBASTIAN

Rabble-rouser! Ignore him. I have this new law which forbids
any—actually if you let me have the ring, it would save the trip.
(TOPHER *tosses the ring.* SEBASTIAN *stamps away.* TOPHER
looks out the window.)

TOPHER

Shouldn't we listen to what he has to say? People were never upset
with Mom and Dad. Were they?

SEBASTIAN

Your parents had the good fortune to be royalty in a time of plenty.
But since their unfortunate demise, I have done my best to run

this country. I've done my best to raise you in the finest schools.

JEAN-MICHEL

Hello, I'm talking here!

TOPHER

We should invite him up for a talk.

SEBASTIAN

Ignore him.

JEAN-MICHEL

I will not give up! If you won't listen, I'll shout this to the town square.

SEBASTIAN

Shout this to the town square—perhaps it's time for a distraction.

TOPHER

What kind of distraction?

SEBASTIAN

A royal wedding.

TOPHER

Wow. And does that work?

SEBASTIAN

Like a dream every time.

TOPHER

But, who will get married?

SEBASTIAN

Well . . . you.

TOPHER

That's just silly. I don't know any girls. I went to an all-boys school off in the woods. And then attended an all-male university, on an island. Why did you do that to me?

SEBASTIAN

For this happy day—I am going to find you a bride—oh, happy the day!

TOPHER

This is nonsense. How will you find me a bride?

SEBASTIAN

We shall have a magnificent ball. Dancing.

TOPHER

What?

SEBASTIAN

Every eligible young woman who can afford a gown will attend. That is a wonderful selection process right there. If you can't afford a nice dress, you don't have any business marrying a prince. Now. All the guests will be in masks. You will dance with every girl. At the stroke of midnight, everyone will remove their masks and you will have found your bride.

TOPHER

That's fast.

SEBASTIAN

King and queen on the throne. I am there to guide you through all your decisions. It's really a win-win.

TOPHER

How would any woman fall in love with me so quickly?

SEBASTIAN

A valid question, which we will answer sometime soon. Now, Lord Pinkleton. I want you to tell this to all—a pronouncement—an announcement.

(LORD PINKLETON *copies down what* SEBASTIAN *speaks.*)

SEBASTIAN

His Royal Highness
Christopher Rupert

TOPHER

Please, don't say my whole name!

SEBASTIAN

Windemere Vladimir

TOPHER

So embarrassing.

SEBASTIAN

Karl Alexander
François Reginald
Launcelot Herman—

LORD PINKLETON & LORDS

Herman?

TOPHER

Herman!

SEBASTIAN

—Gregory James
Is giving a ball!

TOPHER

Sebastian, dancing? Can we talk about this, please?

Scene Four

SCENE: *The Town Square*
(*The* TOWNSPEOPLE *watch as* JEAN-MICHEL *overturns a soap-box and jumps on top of it. He is one voice among many—grunting pigs, screaming* CHILDREN, *arguing* MERCHANTS.)

JEAN-MICHEL

Now is the time,
The time to act,
No other time will do.
Live and play your part
Don't give away your heart
Don't take what the world gives you.
Now is the time,
The time to live,
No other time is real.
Yesterday has gone,
Tomorrow is a guess,
Today you can see and feel.
　　(*Spoken*)
No, no, no, listen. Tradespeople, tinkers, and fishmongers! I shout
to the prince but he ignores me! If he and Sebastian can take the
land of the very poor, it is only a matter of time before they take
from all of us!
　　(*Concerned shouts from the* TOWNSPEOPLE.)

JEAN-MICHEL

For you can't just wait to be served by fate
On a silver plate or a tray.

JEAN-MICHEL & TOWNSPEOPLE
Now is the time,
The time of your life,
The time of your life is today!
(LORD PINKLETON *enters and rings his bell: Ding! Ding!*)

LORD PINKLETON
The Prince is giving a ball!
The Prince is giving a ball!
Hear ye!
Hear ye!
A ball and that's not all!
The Prince is giving a ball!
The Prince is giving a ball!
Hear ye!
Hear ye!
His Royal Highness
Christopher Rupert James
Is giving a ball!

TOWNSPEOPLE
He's giving a ball?

LORD PINKLETON
The Prince is giving a ball!

TOWNSPEOPLE
The Prince is giving a ball!

LORD PINKLETON & TOWNSPEOPLE
The Prince is giving a ball!

JEAN-MICHEL

Hello, I'm talking here!

TOWNSPEOPLE
(*Realizing they've forgotten about* JEAN-MICHEL)

Ohh . . .

JEAN-MICHEL

Now is the time,
The time to act—

TOWNSPEOPLE
(*Hushed*)

He's giving a ball.

JEAN-MICHEL

No other time will do.

TOWNSPEOPLE
(*Hushed*)

The Prince is giving a ball!
(*A* WOMAN *sticks her head out of a window.*)

WOMAN IN WINDOW

He's giving a what?

TOWNSPEOPLE
(*Shouted*)

A ball!!
(JEAN-MICHEL *slams the window shut.*)

JEAN-MICHEL

Now is the time,
The time to live,
No other time is real.

TOWNSPEOPLE

The Prince is giving a—
    (LORD PINKLETON *reveals the invitation*)
Oooh!

LORD PINKLETON

His Royal Highness
Christopher Rupert
Windemere Vladimir
Karl Alexander
François Reginald
Launcelot Herman—

TOWNSPEOPLE

Herman?

LORD PINKLETON

Herman!
Gregory James
Is giving a ball.
    (MADAME *enters, with* GABRIELLE, CHARLOTTE, *and* ELLA.)

MADAME

The Prince is giving a what?

TOWNSPEOPLE

The Prince is giving a ball!

The Prince is giving a ball!

LORD PINKLETON

His Majesty
Has this decree . . .
(*Spoken*)
To attend the ball, all one requires is an invitation and suitably
fashionable attire! And, the Prince shall choose a woman from
the ball to be his bride. That means anyone can be the queen!
(*A* CROWD *gathers around* LORD PINKLETON *as he hands out
invitations. Various* WOMEN *come forward.*)

TALL WOMAN

So will he want a taller girl?

STRONG WOMAN

Or will he want a stronger girl?

SMALL WOMAN

Or will he want a smaller girl?

TOWNSPEOPLE

The Prince is giving a ball!

SHY WOMAN

I wish I were a bolder girl.

OLDER WOMAN

I wish I were a younger girl.

YOUNGER WOMAN

I wish I were an older girl.

TOWNSPEOPLE
The Prince is giving a ball!
(ELLA *comes forward. The* WOMEN *echo her wishes as she sings.*)

ELLA
I've wished a lot of things
I don't wish anymore,
But now I wish a lot of things
I've never wished before.
I wish I had—
I wish I could—
I wish I might—
I wish I would—
I wish I were invited
To the Prince's royal palace ball!
(*The* TOWNSPEOPLE *dance joyously.*)

TOWNSPEOPLE
He's giving a ball!
He's giving a ball!
The Prince is giving a ball!
(*The* TOWNSPEOPLE *continue their dance.*)

JEAN-MICHEL
Now is the time,
The time to act—

TOWNSPEOPLE
We hear ye,
We hear ye, but
The Prince is giving a ball!

JEAN-MICHEL

Now is the time,
The time to live—

TOWNSPEOPLE

We hear ye,
We hear ye, but
His Royal Highness
Christopher Rupert James
Is giving a ball!
—Is giving a ball!
—Is giving a ball!
    (*As they sing, the* TOWNSPEOPLE *usher* JEAN-MICHEL *offstage.*)

LORD PINKLETON

His Royal Highness
Christopher Rupert

TOWNSPEOPLE

Christopher Rupert
Windemere Vladimir

LORD PINKLETON

Slayer of dragons!

TOWNSPEOPLE

Karl Alexander

LORD PINKLETON

Destroyer of gargoyles!

TOWNSPEOPLE
François Reginald

LORD PINKLETON
Sportsman and poet

TOWNSPEOPLE
Launcelot Herman—

LORD PINKLETON
Herman?

TOWNSPEOPLE
Herman!

TOWNSPEOPLE & LORD PINKLETON
Gregory James
Is giving a ball!
(*Overlapping*)
The Prince is giving a ball!
The Prince is giving a ball!
The Prince is giving a ball!
(*All together*)
The Prince is giving a ball!
The Prince is giving a ball!

TOWNSPEOPLE & LORD PINKLETON
The Prince is giving a ball!
A Royal ball!
He's giving a ball!
(*The* TOWNSPEOPLE *dance off with* LORD PINKLETON, *as we transition to the next scene.* MARIE *waddles by.*)

MARIE

Fol-de-rol and fiddledy dee,
Fiddledy faddledy foddle,
All the wishes in the world
Are poppycock and twaddle.
(*The Town Square transforms itself into the interior of* MA-
DAME'*s cottage.* MARIE *is still there.*)

Scene Five

SCENE: *Inside Madame's Cottage*
(MADAME *works on* GABRIELLE'S *hair.* ELLA *tightens* CHAR-LOTTE'S *corset.*)

MARIE
The Prince is giving a ball!
(*Exits.*)

MADAME
Cinderella! When you've finished tightening delicate Charlotte's corset—

CHARLOTTE
Uuhhh. I can taste my lunch.

MADAME
—we must move on to Gabrielle's hair. It is beginning to look, I fear, like a Bavarian pretzel. Cinderella! Cinderella— (*Stops and chuckles*) Cinderella, it is a most amusing name. I crack myself up. She sits by the cinders of the fire, and her name is Ella. So I call her Cinder-ella. (*Becomes overcome with laughter, then says in her sigh*) Why don't I have any friends?

CHARLOTTE
Face it, Mama, you are well-versed in the art of ridicule.

MADAME
I do have a flair for it, don't I, actual daughters? Watch and learn! (ELLA *reenters*) Cinderella, hurry, get dressed, get ready for the ball, you're going to find a husband!

CHARLOTTE

Am I?

MADAME

Ridicule—who caught it?

CHARLOTTE

I did.

GABRIELLE

That's terrible.
(*A knock on the door.*)

MADAME

Who can that be and at this hour? Everyone clear out of here while I get rid of this imbecile. Cinderella, get that dress on Charlotte!
(ELLA, GABRIELLE, *and* CHARLOTTE *exit.* MADAME *approaches the door. Another knock.*)

MADAME

What brand of idiot would—
(MADAME *swings open the door, revealing* SEBASTIAN. *Her affect changes to warm.*)

MADAME

Why, Sebastian, what an unexpected delight.

SEBASTIAN

Madame, I have but a moment. I invite you to hang upon my every word.

MADAME

Invitation accepted.

SEBASTIAN

Tonight's ball shall be in masks. The Prince will be in the white mask. What color mask will your daughter Gabrielle be wearing?

MADAME

Why, pink.

SEBASTIAN

If the daughter is anything like the mother, I think the pink mask and the white mask should meet and fall in love.

MADAME

Are you implying what I am inferring?

SEBASTIAN

Your daughter is all part of my master plan.

MADAME

You are brilliant.

SEBASTIAN

You are perceptive. I shall see you at the ball. Together we shall make this so.
(*Exits.*)

MADAME

Come daughters, come!
(ELLA, CHARLOTTE, *and* GABRIELLE *run on.*)
Oh Gabrielle, my Gabrielle, just look at you. You too, Charlotte,

but really look at Gabrielle! Cinderella, fetch the orange box.
(ELLA *quickly does so.* MADAME *opens the box.* ALL *gasp in amazement.* MADAME *pulls a tiny elegant piece of Venetian glass from the box.*)

MADAME

From Venice—a piece of glass, spun to perfection. More valuable than diamonds. Each of us shall wear the tiniest bit of hand-blown Venetian glass. Allow me to place this tiny bauble around the neck of my courageous Charlotte.
(*Placing glass around* CHARLOTTE's *neck*)
Allow me to place this tiny bauble around the neck of my beautiful daughter Gabrielle.
(*Placing glass around* GABRIELLE's *neck*)
Cinderella, fetch the perfume! Come two daughters that count, finish getting ready!
 . (*A knock at the door*)
Who can that be? It must be good news!
(MADAME *opens the door, revealing* JEAN-MICHEL, *with two small bouquets.*)

JEAN-MICHEL

Good evening, Madame. Gabrielle? Please forgive me for interrupting your momentous evening. For the ball tonight, I thought you might desire to take these wild flowers. I've picked them myself.
(JEAN-MICHEL *hands* GABRIELLE *the flowers.*)

GABRIELLE

Thank you, Jean-Michel. They're so beautiful. .

JEAN-MICHEL
(*Hands second bouquet to* MADAME)
For the mother of the most perfect girl in all God's creation. I
have gathered these myself and—

MADAME
You are not welcome here! Out of my house!

JEAN-MICHEL
Would you perhaps consider—
(MADAME *takes* GABRIELLE's *flowers and throws them back to*
JEAN-MICHEL.)

MADAME
Leave!
(*Slams door in his face, shouts through window*)
And take your simple pleasures with you.

GABRIELLE
Madame, don't be mean. That was so nice.

MADAME
No, no. No, no, no. Plans. There are plans. Plans that do not
include Mr. Soapbox.

GABRIELLE
But he means well and I think he likes me.

MADAME
Let me tell you about love, Miss Flowers-in-your-hand-and-
dreams-in-your-head. I married your father for love. He died
and I cried. Then I married Cinderella's father for money. He

died. I got a house.

(*A cuckoo clock chimes*)

Seven-thirty! Ball preparation, double time!

(*A series of mad dashes, in final preparation for the ball, begins.*)

MADAME

Cinderella, my shoes!

(ELLA *polishes her shoes*)

Charlotte, powder your sister's face!

(CHARLOTTE *powders* GABRIELLE'*s face and covers her glasses
with powder.*)

GABRIELLE

I can't see!

MADAME

Venetian glass!

(ELLA *places the Venetian glass necklace on* MADAME'*s neck.*)

CHARLOTTE

I'm hungry.

MADAME

Gabrielle, feed the baby!

(GABRIELLE *puts a large biscuit in* CHARLOTTE'*s mouth*)

Cinderella, my cloak.

ELLA

Coming Madame.

MADAME

Expensive bracelet, necklace, hair. Then the Prince we shall
ensnare.

GABRIELLE & CHARLOTTE

Then the Prince we shall ensnare.

MADAME

Are we worthy?

GABRIELLE & CHARLOTTE

Yes. Yes!

MADAME

To battle! The crown is ours to lose! Posture. Posture.
(MADAME, GABRIELLE, *and* CHARLOTTE *exit the house.* CIN-
DERELLA *follows with the invitations. The scene continues as
the location transitions.*)

Scene Six

SCENE: *Outside Madame's Cottage*

GABRIELLE & CHARLOTTE
Expensive bracelet, necklace, hair. Then the Prince we shall ensnare.

GABRIELLE
(*Realizing they've forgotten their invitations*)
Invitations!
(MADAME, GABRIELLE, *and* CHARLOTTE *circle back to* ELLA, *who already has the invitations ready.*)

MADAME
Let us storm the castle, lovely daughters. This is the night everything changes! Now off to the ball!
(*The mad dash ends, with* MADAME, GABRIELLE, *and* CHARLOTTE *fully dressed in the yard, with invitations in hand. They exit, leaving* ELLA. JEAN-MICHEL *enters from behind a tree, touching his bleeding lip.*)

JEAN-MICHEL
One of the flowers in the bouquet was a wild rose. Its thorn has scratched my lip. Yes—I'm bleeding. I should walk up to the prince, scratch his lip.

ELLA
Oh now.

JEAN-MICHEL
Make him drink lemonade, oh it will sting!

ELLA

That's just cruel.

JEAN-MICHEL

Enough of taking things as they are, now is the time for us to march to the palace—the peasants, the tradespeople—and finally get the Prince to listen to us. Instead of having his fancy ball!

ELLA

You should do that, you should march up to him and talk to him!

JEAN-MICHEL

He won't listen to me, he uses his castle to hide from the truth. Him meeting me will never happen! The only thing funnier is you going to the ball. Ha! Why don't you just go to the ball and ask the Prince when he's going to start noticing? Noticing that the people are being evicted from their land. Ha! That's absurd. Ha!
    (*Exits.*)

ELLA

Jean-Michel! I could go to the Prince and he might listen to me! And if I had a ball gown, I think I might look sort of nice.
    I am in the royal palace, of all places!
    When I meet the finest Prince you've ever seen,
    And the color on my two stepsisters' faces
    Is a queer sort of sour-apple green.
    I am coy and flirtatious
    When alone with the prince.
    I'm the belle of the ball
    In my own little corner
    All alone
    In my own

Little chair.

MARIE

(*Entering from behind tree*)
Fol-de-rol and fiddledy dee,
Fiddledy faddledy foddle,
All the wishes in the world
Are poppycock and twaddle!

ELLA

Oh Crazy Marie. Are you mocking me with your gibberish?

MARIE

Yes.
   (*Sings*)
Fol-de-rol and fiddledy dee,
Fiddledy faddledy foodle,
All the dreamers in all the world
Are dizzy in the noodle.

ELLA

So what if I do have a dream to see the Prince again? And tell him what life in his kingdom is really like? And what it could be.

MARIE

Exactly. And then to have him fall in love with you.

ELLA

No one will fall in love with me. Why do you come to visit me tonight?

MARIE
I just knew I would find you
In the same little chair
In the pale pink mist of a foolish dream.

ELLA
I am being foolish.

MARIE
Then be foolish with me. What would you dream of?

ELLA
Why, an invitation to the ball, I guess.

MARIE
(*Produces invitation*)
Right here. There's an invitation.

ELLA
What? But it's torn.

MARIE
Don't wait for everything to be perfect, just go! Now, what else
would you dream of?

ELLA
Oh, a white gown, I imagine. A beautiful white gown sewn up
with pearls. And jewels. And a tiara of diamonds.

MARIE
And on your feet?

ELLA

Why, the most beautiful grosgrain pumps, I'd imagine.

MARIE

No. Better. The Venetian glass that your stepmother so loves in her trinkets and baubles. An entire pair of shoes made only of Venetian glass.

ELLA

Oh, how silly. I'd be the envy of all. But how would I get to the ball?

MARIE

Well, that pumpkin over there?

ELLA

Yes?

MARIE

I'll turn it into a golden carriage.

ELLA

And horses?

MARIE

Those mice? Trapped in the cage.

ELLA

And a fox as a footman, and a raccoon as a driver. Oh, you are crazy, Marie. Why, in order to do that, you would have to be a fairy godmother.

(MARIE *rips off her rags and ragged cape. Underneath is the most beautiful gown.* ELLA *gasps.*)

ELLA

Marie! But you're a crazy woman! What are you doing in that beautiful gown?

MARIE

You'd be surprised how many beautiful gowns have crazy women in them.

ELLA

Are you really my fairy godmother?

MARIE

But of course, my child. Actually, I'm everyone's fairy godmother. But you're the only one who's given me charity. Generosity. And kindness. And now, I must make all the dreams we joked about come true.

ELLA

But that's so improbable. Implausible.

MARIE

Impossible
For a plain yellow pumpkin
To become a golden carriage!
Impossible
For a plain country bumpkin
And a prince to join in marriage!
And four white mice will never be four white horses—
Such fol-de-rol and fiddledy dee of course is
Impossible!

But the world is full of zanies and fools
Who don't believe in sensible rules
And won't believe what sensible people say,
And because these daft and dewy-eyed dopes
Keep building up impossible hopes,
Impossible things are happ'ning every day!

ELLA

Impossible!

MARIE

Impossible!

ELLA

Impossible!

MARIE

Impossible!

ELLA

Impossible!

MARIE

Impossible!

ELLA & MARIE

Impossible!

ELLA

But if you could be a beggar woman not five minutes ago and
now are my fairy godmother, then anything is possible, right?

MARIE

I suppose so.

ELLA

You could change it all. You could make it all happen.

MARIE

No, but you could change it. You could make it all happen.

ELLA

Never. I couldn't.

MARIE

You're right. It's all so—
(*Sings*)
Impossible
For a plain yellow pumpkin
To become a golden carriage!
Impossible
For a plain country bumpkin
And a prince to join in marriage!
And four white mice will never be four white horses—
Such fol-de-rol and fiddledy dee of course is
Impossible!

ELLA

But the world is full of zanies and fools
Who don't believe in sensible rules
And won't believe what sensible people say,

ELLA & MARIE

And because these daft and dewy-eyed dopes

Keep building up impossible hopes,
Impossible things are happ'ning every day!
(MARIE *casts a spell on the pumpkin and the pumpkin blows*
up like a balloon. The "leaves" peel away. The pumpkin ex-
plodes and the carriage is revealed. MARIE *scoops up the mice*
in the cage. She flings them into the air and a team of horses
appears from the wings. MARIE *crosses to the porch, playfully*
approaches the FOX, *who has appeared in the woodbin. She*
points at the FOX, *indicating "You're next." The* FOX *shakes*
his head. MARIE *casts a spell on the* FOX, *who quickly ducks*
into the woodbin. The FOOTMAN *tumbles out of the woodbin*
in a state of surprise. The FOOTMAN *straightens his knees. The*
FOOTMAN *shakes his head.* MARIE *casts a spell upon the* RAC-
COON, *who hides in the tree. The* COACHMAN *pops out from*
the tree. The COACHMAN *scampers down from the tree and*
stands on two feet. The FOOTMAN *and* COACHMAN *regard one*
another. The FOOTMAN *and the* COACHMAN *shake their legs*
and walk upstage. MARIE *casts a spell upon* ELLA, *who whirls*
about. As she whirls the dress changes from rags to a beautiful
crown. ELLA'*s dress transformation is complete. She is now in*
a beautiful white gown and tiara.)

ELLA
It's the most beautiful gown in all the land!

MARIE
And as promised, in our laughter . . . glass slippers.
(MARIE *holds up the glass shoes, places them on the ground, and*
ELLA *eases into them*)
But Cinderella—I must tell you—all of this magic is very power-
ful, but it will end at midnight tonight. Now go—to the ball. In
the name of every girl who has ever wished to go to a ball in a

beautiful dress. In the name of every girl who has ever wanted to change the world she lived in. Go! With the promise of possibility!

Scene Seven

SCENE: *Flight to the Castle*
(ELLA *climbs in the carriage. The carriage rides across the treetops.*)

ELLA

It's possible!
It's possible!
It's possible!
It's possible!
It's possible!
It's possible!
It's possible!

For a plain yellow pumpkin
To become a golden carriage!
It's possible
For a plain country bumpkin
And a prince to join in marriage!
And four white mice are easily turned to horses—
Such fol-de-rol and fiddledy dee of course is
Quite possible!

MARIE

For the world is full of zanies and fools
Who don't believe in sensible rules

ELLA

And won't believe what sensible people say,
(MARIE *appears, flying over* ELLA.)

MARIE & ELLA

And because these daft and dewy-eyed dopes
Keep building up impossible hopes,
Impossible things are happ'ning every day!

ELLA

It's possible!

MARIE

It's possible!

ELLA

It's possible!

MARIE

It's possible!

ELLA

It's possible!

MARIE

It's possible!

ELLA

It's possible!.
(*The carriage arrives at the palace. The* DRIVER *and* FOOTMAN *help* ELLA *out.* MARIE *flies off.* ELLA *enters the palace.*)

Scene Eight

SCENE: *The Castle Ballroom*
(*The* LADIES *dance on.* TOPHER *enters.* SEBASTIAN *and* LORD
PINKLETON *enter.*)

TOPHER

Sebastian, honestly!

SEBASTIAN

Only two hundred to go!
(*The* LORDS *dance on.* MADAME *enters, with* GABRIELLE *and*
CHARLOTTE. *The gavotte begins.* TOPHER *and* CHARLOTTE
dance.)

CHARLOTTE

So which one is it?

TOPHER

Which one is which?

CHARLOTTE

Duh. The Prince. Which is the Prince, I mean come on!?! What
do you think I'm here for, the free food?

TOPHER

Well, a good time, a dance perhaps?

CHARLOTTE

Wrong answer! I got marrying royalty on my mind. So which
one is he here?

TOPHER
Well, maybe it's me.

CHARLOTTE
(*A moment of thought, then*)
Not likely. You're no Prince, you're ordinary.

TOPHER
What makes you think I'm ordinary?

CHARLOTTE
We're doing a gavotte and you can't even keep the beat. When we get to the waltz, you're gonna trip over your two left feet and land on your flat little bottom. End of discussion.

TOPHER
Hope to talk to you later.

CHARLOTTE
I've moved on.
(CHARLOTTE *crosses to* PINKLETON, *grabs the mallet, and bangs the gong, walking away in disgust.* MADAME *pushes* TOPHER'*s next* PARTNER *away, placing* GABRIELLE *in her place.*)

NEXT PARTNER
Hey!

TOPHER
How do you do?

GABRIELLE
How do you do?

TOPHER

A lovely dance isn't it? I hope my dancing is all right.

GABRIELLE

Oh, your dancing is absolutely princely—oops, I let that slip out.

TOPHER

Ahh, so you know.

GABRIELLE

I would know a wise and handsome Prince anywhere.

TOPHER

The last girl did not know.
(MADAME *glides by* CHARLOTTE *and whispers in her ear.*)

CHARLOTTE

You're kidding!! Well thanks for the heads up! Ugh!!!

GABRIELLE

I think she does now.

TOPHER

Well.

GABRIELLE

So.

TOPHER

What can you tell me about yourself?

GABRIELLE

What would it please you to know, Your Highness?

TOPHER

OK. Creepy.

CHARLOTTE

Your Majestic Highness, just because I was playing hard to get doesn't mean I'm hard to get!

TOPHER

Really creepy. Sebastian, I can't do this anymore, I'm sorry.

A DUCHESS

It's the Prince!

(*The* LADIES *throw themselves at* TOPHER, *pushing and pulling him about the dance floor. Just as the gavotte ends,* ELLA *appears.* EVERYONE *in the ballroom freezes at the sight of her, struck by her tremendous beauty.* TOPHER *sees* ELLA. *The* CROWD *parts.* TOPHER *bows.* ELLA *curtsies.* TOPHER *offers his hand.*)

SEBASTIAN

It's time to play Ridicule! Everyone! Take sides!

(ELLA *is taken from* TOPHER *by a* COURTIER *and two circles form as the* MEMBERS OF THE COURT *dance to the Ridicule theme.* SEBASTIAN *grabs* TOPHER *and pulls him forward to talk to him.*)

TOPHER

What happened to the nice girl?

SEBASTIAN

Ignore her. We're playing Ridicule, you get to be judge. Two circles spin and when the music stops two players out-ridicule one another. Let's find you a bride.

GUESTS

Bum ditty bum bum.
Bum ditty bum bum.

LORD PINKLETON

One and two and three!
(*The music stops. An* OLDER WOMAN *is stopped in front of* CHARLOTTE.)

OLDER WOMAN

Oh, but my dear. I love that dress. No matter how many times I see it.
(*The room "ooos" and applauds*)
Why I remember when that dress was first in fashion, when I was a young girl—

CHARLOTTE

Please do not speak of your childhood, as I have not brought along a copy of the Old Testament to follow along.
(SEBASTIAN *tells* TOPHER *to indicate that the victory goes to* CHARLOTTE. TOPHER *does so and the* CROWD *responds with* "Brava," "Touché," *etc. The* CROWD *begins to dance again.* SEBASTIAN *pulls* TOPHER *forward again.*)

TOPHER

What do you even call that?

SEBASTIAN

Well, it's awfully sophisticated.

TOPHER

It just seems like cruelty.

SEBASTIAN

Sophisticated, cruelty. There's a slight difference there, I keep forgetting what it is.

TOPHER

I'm not quite sure I want to play this game.

SEBASTIAN

And here we have another round at the ready!

GUESTS

Bum ditty bum bum.
Bum ditty bum bum.

LORD PINKLETON

One and two and three!
(*Music stops.* MADAME *and* ELLA *must face off.*)

MADAME

Age before beauty. You first, dear.
(*"Ooohs" from the crowd.*)

ELLA

You have such a beautiful speaking voice. Have you ever considered reciting poetry?
(*Silence and muttering from the crowd.*)

MADAME
(*Cracking*)

Say it—what—do it—what?! The anticipation is killing me! Do the Ridicule! Why do you say that?

ELLA

No reason. I just really like your speaking voice and I just think you would sound really wonderful reciting a poem. And I also like the feather in your hair. It's a lovely color for you.

MADAME

Why. Are. You. Doing this. To. Meeee?!!

SEBASTIAN

What is this bewitchery you practice?

ELLA

It's just kindness.

SEBASTIAN

Kind-ness?

ELLA

Oh yes. Kindness is practiced now in all the great courts. Ridicule isn't done anywhere anymore. It's all kindness now. Even in the French courts.

SEBASTIAN

Kind-ness.

ELLA

Yes. You know. Compassion.

SEBASTIAN

Who are you, you strange woman?

MADAME

I don't know who she is but she is very, very wealthy indeed. And did you see her feet? Shoes made of Venetian glass! My resentment is all-consuming.

ELLA

Kindness. You must all try it.
(*A murmuring from the crowd.* "No." "I don't think so." "Not I." "I won't be the first.")

TOPHER

I'll be the first. Kindness. Isn't it wonderful to have a pleasant young lady such as yourself in our court?

ELLA

Thank you. And it's an honor to be at this wonderful party you are throwing.

SEBASTIAN

It's like every time they speak a part of me dies.
(*A* LORD *steps forward.*)

A LORD

This room is filled with some of the loveliest women I have ever seen.
(*A* LADY *steps forward.*)

A LADY

I just saw they have vanilla cake on the buffet. I love vanilla cake!

Thank you to whoever made it!

A GUEST

This court is alive with laughter and warmth.

ANOTHER GUEST

It's like it was during the reign of Prince Topher's parents!

A DIGNITARY

May his reign be a continuation of theirs!

A DUCHESS

Those were glorious days.

ANOTHER GUEST

But so are these.

YET ANOTHER DUCHESS

Look at these magnificent guests! Ha ha!!

GABRIELLE

(*Steps forward and says to* ELLA, *grabbing her hand*)
You are so kind—thank you. You make me wish I were a better person. There's something somewhat familiar about you. What could that be?
(ELLA *turns to get away from* GABRIELLE. *There is* TOPHER.)

TOPHER

I admire how you've changed everything around. And yet, I'm so comfortable with you. I feel as if I've met you before.
(*Sings*)
Ten minutes ago, I saw you.

I looked up when you came through the door.
My head started reeling;
You gave me the feeling
The room had no ceiling or floor.

Ten minutes ago, I met you,
And we murmured our how-do-you-do's.
I wanted to ring out the bells
And fling out my arms
And to sing out the news:

I have found her!
She's an angel,
With the dust of the stars in her eyes!
We are dancing!
We are flying!
And she's taking me back to the skies.

In the arms of my love I'm flying
Over mountain and meadow and glen,
And I like it so well
That for all I can tell
I may never come down again!
I may never come down to earth again!
     (*Spoken*)
I'm sorry to be so effusive, I've just met you. I'm not usually this
way with someone I've just met. Events like this . . . I just feel
like—what am I doing here?

ELLA

I feel the same.

TOPHER

Like such a phony.

ELLA

So do I!

TOPHER

You do?

ELLA

Yes!

TOPHER

Me too! My name is—

ELLA

Topher, short for Christopher. Yes, I know.

TOPHER

Have we met before?

ELLA

Yes, and we are seeing each other for the first time right now.
　　(*Sings*)
　　Ten minutes ago, I met you,
　　And we murmured our how-do-you-do's.
　　I wanted to ring out the bells
　　And fling out my arms
　　And to sing out the news:
　　I have found him!
　　I have found him!
　　　　(TOPHER *and* ELLA *dance together*)

In the arms of my love I'm flying
Over mountain and meadow and glen,
And I like it so well
That for all I can tell
I may never come down again!

TOPHER & ELLA
I may never come down to earth again!

TOPHER, ELLA & CHORUS
(*Singing in beautiful counterpoint harmony*)
Ten minutes ago, I met you,
And we murmured our how-do-you-do's.
I wanted to ring out the bells
And fling out my arms
And to sing out the news:
I have found her!
She's an angel,
With the dust of the stars in her eyes!
We are dancing!
We are flying!
And she's taking me back to the skies!
In the arms of my love I'm flying
Over mountain and meadow and glen,
And I like it so well
That for all I can tell
I may never come down again!
I may never come down to earth again!
    (*They kiss.*)

ELLA
I have to go!

TOPHER

But I've just found you!

ELLA

I don't want to go, but I must!

TOPHER

Don't go!

ELLA

Prince Topher. There's something I must tell you. You need to open your eyes to what's happening in your kingdom. The poor are having their land taken. You must help them. You must.

TOPHER

I don't think that's kind. How can you say that's kindness?

ELLA

This is all so wonderful! You are so wonderful, but I have to go!
(ELLA *runs away and is lost in the* CROWD.)

TOPHER

Wait! Young Lady! Where are you going?! Wait! Stop!

SEBASTIAN

Your Highness! Your Highness!

MADAME

Charlotte! Gabrielle!
(*The* GUESTS *dance off as the scene transitions.*)

Scene Nine

SCENE: *The Palace Steps*
(ELLA *runs down the staircase. The* PRINCE *appears at the top of the stairs.* ELLA *trips and falls, losing one of her glass slippers.* ELLA *stands up.* TOPHER *and* ELLA *look at each other.* ELLA *runs back up, grabs her shoe, and runs into the carriage, which rides away. The* PRINCE *is left standing.*)

TOPHER
Wait! Wait! I don't even know your name?!

(*The curtain falls. End of Act One.*)

ACT TWO

Scene One

TOPHER

Wait! Wait! I don't even know your name?!
(*A* CROWD, *including* SEBASTIAN, MADAME, GABRIELLE, *and* CHARLOTTE, *rushes on*)
She has run off! The lady—we must find her, she left in a golden carriage! After her!!

SEBASTIAN

Madame, we will take your carriage!

MADAME

We haven't the room!

SEBASTIAN

Leave one of your daughters behind then!

TOPHER

After her, she is my destiny!!!
(TOPHER *and the* KNIGHTS *run off.* SEBASTIAN *leaves with* MADAME *and* GABRIELLE. CHARLOTTE *and the other* LADIES *of the court are left, on the steps of the palace.*)

CHARLOTTE

But—But—
(*Looks at the other* LADIES)
No, seriously, what just happened? Seriously?
(*The* LADIES *sit on the steps and take off their shoes.*)

CHARLOTTE

Why would a fellow want a girl like her,
A frail and fluffy beauty?
Why can't a fellow ever once prefer
A solid girl like me?

She's a frothy little bubble
With a flimsy kind of charm
And with very little trouble
I could break her little arm!

(CHARLOTTE *squeezes a* LADY's *arm.*)

FIRST LADY

Ow! Ow!!

CHARLOTTE

Why would a fellow want a girl like her,
So obviously unusual?
Why can't a fellow ever once prefer
A usual girl like me?

SECOND LADY

Her cheeks are a pretty shade of pink,

CHARLOTTE

But not any pinker than a rose is.

THIRD LADY

Her skin may be delicate and soft,

CHARLOTTE

But not any softer than a doe's is.

FOURTH LADY

Her neck is no whiter than a swan's.

FIRST LADY

She's only as dainty as a daisy.

CHARLOTTE

She's only as graceful as a bird,
So why is the fellow going crazy?

CHARLOTTE & LADIES

Oh, why would a fellow want a girl like her,
A girl who's merely lovely?
Why can't a fellow ever once prefer
A girl who's merely me?
What's the matter with the man?
What's the matter with the man?
What's the matter with the man?
    (CHARLOTTE *throws her shoe offstage.* SEBASTIAN *and* LORD
    PINKLETON *enter.*)

SEBASTIAN

Footwear is now falling from the sky!
    (TOPHER *and the* KNIGHTS *reenter.*)

TOPHER

It's gone—the golden carriage has taken a shortcut right through
the forest. Gentlemen, lanterns!! We must find her if it's the last
thing we do—she is my lady!!!
    (TOPHER *runs off with the* KNIGHTS *into the castle.* CHARLOTTE
    takes this all in.)

CHARLOTTE

Yes, he's witty,
So disarming,
And I really like the way he holds a room.
Clever, cunning,
Ever charming,
How do I make him see I'm special?
It's a pity,

LADIES

It's a pity,

CHARLOTTE

I'm as pretty,

LADIES

I'm as pretty,
Plus I've got the patience
Of a perfect saint.

CHARLOTTE & LADIES

So I'm waiting,
Always waiting,
Nevertheless,
I'm in a mess.

CHARLOTTE

Loosen my dress
Help me, I'm starting to faint!

LADIES
Why would a fellow want a girl like her,
A girl who isn't dizzy?
Why can't a fellow ever once prefer

CHARLOTTE
A high-strung girl like me?
Her cheeks are a pretty shade of pink,

LADIES
What's the matter with the man?

CHARLOTTE
But not any pinker than a rose is.

LADIES
What's the matter with the man?

CHARLOTTE
Her skin may be delicate and soft,

LADIES
What's the matter with the man?

CHARLOTTE
But not any softer than a doe's is.
Her neck is no whiter than a swan's.

LADIES
What's the matter with the man?

CHARLOTTE
She's only as dainty as a daisy.

LADIES
What's the matter with the man?

CHARLOTTE
She's only as graceful as a bird,

LADIES
What's the matter?

CHARLOTTE & LADIES
So why is the fellow going crazy?
Oh, oh,
Why would a fellow want a girl like her,
A girl who's merely lovely?
Why can't a fellow ever once prefer
A girl who's merely me?

LADIES
What's the matter with the man?
What's the matter with the man?
What's the matter with the man?

CHARLOTTE
She's the matter—
Let me at her!

Opening Night: March 3rd, 2013, Broadway Theater, Douglas Carter Beane and
Mark Brokaw holding photo of Rodgers + Hammerstein, with Laura Osnes.

Laura Osnes, Broadway, 2013.

Santino Fontana, with his Knights and Heralds, Broadway, 2013.

Victoria Clark, Broadway, 2013.

Harriet Harris, Broadway, 2013.

Laura Osnes and company, "The Prince is Giving a Ball", Broadway, 2013.

Ann Harada and the Ladies of the Court, "Stepsister's Lament", Broadway, 2013.

(From left to right) Harriet Harris, Ann Harada, Marla Mindelle, and Laura Osnes, "A Lovely Night", Broadway, 2013.

Laura Osnes, Santino Fontana and company, "Cinderella Waltz", Broadway, 2013.

Santino Fontana and Laura Osnes, "The Shoe Fits", Broadway, 2013.

You make your bow
And smile somehow
And shily answer "yes" -

Stepmother

How would you know
That this is so?

Cinderella

(Humbly)

I do no more than guess.

Joy and Portia

(Singing loud like two very devout choir
singers)

You can guess till you're blue in the face
But you can't even picture such a man.

Joy

He is _more_ than a Prince -

Portia

He's an _Ace_!

Cinderella

But sisters, I really think I can -

Stepmother

Can what?

Cinderella

I think I can picture such a man ....

Joy and Portia

(Reverently starting to sing a hymn to
his charms)

He is tall -

Notations by Richard Rodgers on his copy of the original script, indicating the rhythm he planned, and eventually used, for "When You're Driving Through the Moonlight."

Lesley Ann Warren in the 1965 CBS remake.

(From left to right) Pat Carroll, Ginger Rogers, Barbara Ruick , Lesley Ann
Warren, Celeste Holm, Stuart Damon, Jo Van Fleet, and Walter Pidgeon in
the 1965 CBS remake.

Julie Andrews, Oscar Hammerstein II, and Richard Rodgers during preparations for the 1957 CBS telecast.

Julie Andrews—the original Cinderella.

Brandy Norwood and Whitney Houston in the 1997 ABC remake.

LADIES

What's the matter with the man?
What's the matter with the man?
What's the matter with the man?

CHARLOTTE

What's the matter with the man?
   (CHARLOTTE *and the* LADIES *exit.*)

Scene Two

SCENE: *The Forest*
(*Outside the palace, a bugle sounds. The* KNIGHTS *enter with* LORD PINKLETON, *bugle in hand.*)

LORD PINKLETON
Your Majesty, Your Majesty.

TOPHER
(*Entering*)
Lord Pinkleton, where is she?

LORD PINKLETON
There are reports along the eastern road of a golden carriage.

TOPHER
Ten minutes ago, I held her . . .
(LORD PINKLETON *sounds his bugle again. Two* DUKES *enter.*)

DUKE OF CAVENDISH
Your Majesty, we saw the carriage! And this I cannot explain—it simply flew into the mist!

DUKE OF CHESHIRE
Impossible I know—

TOPHER
Impossible! Then we shall do the impossible!
(*The* DUKES *exit.* TOPHER *sings to himself*)
Ten minutes ago . . .
(*One by one, the other* KNIGHTS *enter with their lanterns*)

We were dancing in the palace of all places,
And her gown was like a cloud of snowy white.
How the moonlight shone its beams upon our faces,
'Til she vanished like a phantom in the night.
I just know I will find you,
You're the girl of my dreams
And the thrill is more than my heart can bear . . .

LORD PINKLETON

Look, a carriage!

TOPHER

That's it! That's the one! After her!!

(TOPHER *and the* KNIGHTS *venture into the woods, lanterns into hand. A flash of smoke, then the* FOOTMAN *and the* DRIVER *roll onstage along with the now untransformed pumpkin.* ELLA *enters and grabs the pumpkin. The* TRIO *are chased by* TO-PHER *and the* KNIGHTS. *Hijinks ensue! The* KNIGHTS *grab the* FOOTMAN. *They struggle. The* FOOTMAN *jumps into a hollowed log. A* KNIGHT *reaches in to pull him out, but instead finds himself holding the untransformed* FOX. *The* KNIGHT *screams and throws the* FOX *offstage. More* KNIGHTS *enter, chasing the* DRIVER. *They chase him round a tree several times. The* DRIVER *climbs into the tree, and the untransformed* RACCOON *emerges. The* KNIGHTS *head off elsewhere.*)

Scene Three

SCENE: *Outside, then Inside, Madame's Cottage*
(ELLA *runs on, out of breath, still clutching the pumpkin. She hears* TOPHER *and his* KNIGHTS. ELLA *hides behind a small wall. The* KNIGHTS *and* TOPHER *enter, looking for her, coming close to finding her. Then, they turn their attention elsewhere.*)

TOPHER

To the west!

> (TOPHER *and the* KNIGHTS *exit. The magic wears off, and* ELLA'*s dress disappears. She is back in her provincial outfit.*)

ELLA

He was tall, very tall,
And his eyes were clear and blue.
> (*The sound of* TOPHER *and his* KNIGHTS *searching.* ELLA *hides*)
He was slim, very slim.
In his coat of snowy hue.
> (*Louder noises from* TOPHER *and his* KNIGHTS. ELLA *sits on the stool*)
When he walked across the ballroom floor,
He was like a thing divine;
And all the ladies turned their heads,
And natur'lly I turned mine.
The chandeliers were shooting stars,
The drums and horns and soft guitars
Were sounding more like nightingales;
The window curtains blew like sails,
And I was floating just above the floor,
Feeling slightly taller than before.
> (*During this verse, the exterior of the cottage has transformed into the interior.* ELLA *is now in the cottage*)

He was tall, very tall . . .
(*The door swings open. In strides* MADAME.)

MADAME

When I left this house in my carriage, I was quite convinced my
daughter was going to be queen and I would never have to come
back here to this. And now, well, I'm back here to this.

ELLA

Was the ball a disappointment, Madame?

MADAME

The Prince, despite his being well born, and raised with great
care by our Lord Protector, showed the most appalling manners.
Appalling! He spent the entire evening talking and dancing with
some little nobody.

ELLA

How did Gabrielle and Charlotte take that?
(*The door swings open.* CHARLOTTE *enters, dejected.* GABRIELLE
follows.)

CHARLOTTE

The Prince has fallen head over heels for someone else. If he keeps
this up, I may not want to go out with him!

MADAME

What was going on in His Royal Highness's thick skull?

CHARLOTTE

The way he looked at her. With respect! I hope no man ever looks
at me that way.

MADAME

If that woman had any morality or sense of what's right in this world, she would not have appeared at the ball at all.

GABRIELLE

But can you imagine how she must have felt tonight, arriving at the ball and meeting the man of her dreams?

MADAME

I cannot, for my mind has no place for the puerile or rank.

GABRIELLE

I can imagine it, I think.

ELLA

I can imagine it.

CHARLOTTE

I can imagine it, and I have no imagination.

ELLA

When you're driving through the moonlight on the highway,
When you're driving through the moonlight to the dance,
You are breathless with a wild anticipation
Of adventure and excitement and romance.
Then at last you see the towers of the palace
Silhouetted on the sky above the park,
And below them is a row of lighted windows,
Like a lovely diamond necklace in the dark!

CHARLOTTE

It looks that way—

GABRIELLE

The way you say.

MADAME

She talks as if she knows.

ELLA

I do not know
These things are so.
I only just suppose . . .
I suppose that when you come into the ballroom,
And the room itself is floating in the air,
If you're suddenly confronted by His Highness
You are frozen like a statue on the stair!
You're afraid he'll hear the way your heart is beating
And you know you mustn't make the first advance.
You are seriously thinking of retreating—
Then you seem to hear him asking you to dance!
You make a bow,
A timid bow,
And shyly answer "yes."

MADAME

How would you know
That this is so?

ELLA

I do no more than guess.

CHARLOTTE & GABRIELLE

You can guess 'til you're blue in the face,
But you can't even picture such a man.

CHARLOTTE

He is more than a prince—

GABRIELLE

He's an ace!

ELLA

But sisters, I really think I can—

MADAME
(*Spoken*)

Can what?

ELLA

I think that I can picture such a man

CHARLOTTE & GABRIELLE

He is tall—

ELLA

And straight as a lance!

CHARLOTTE & GABRIELLE

And his hair—

ELLA

Is dark and wavy!

CHARLOTTE & GABRIELLE

His eyes—

ELLA

Can melt you with a glance!

CHARLOTTE & GABRIELLE

He can turn a girl to gravy!

ELLA

(*Spoken*)

And I can imagine it.

GABRIELLE

I imagine it too!

CHARLOTTE

This squinting isn't my sinus condition. It's me imagining it.

MADAME

I am throwing caution to the wind! I am imagining it as well!

ELLA

Imagine what that girl would be feeling when dancing with the
Prince!
　　(*Sings*)
　　A lovely night,
　　A lovely night,
　　A finer night you know you'll never see.
　　You meet your prince,
　　A charming prince,
　　As charming as a prince will ever be!
　　The stars in a hazy heaven
　　Tremble above you
　　While he is whispering,

"Darling, I love you!"
You say goodbye,
Away you fly,
But on your lips you keep a kiss,
All your life you'll dream of this
Lovely, lovely night.

MADAME

Charlotte, play the pianoforte.

CHARLOTTE

Okay, but it's not going to be good.
(ELLA *pulls out the pianoforte, which* CHARLOTTE *plays.*)

CHARLOTTE

A lovely night,
A lovely night,
A finer night you know you'll never see.

GABRIELLE

La, la, la

CHARLOTTE

La, la, la

CHARLOTTE & GABRIELLE

La, la, la

CHARLOTTE, GABRIELLE, MADAME, ELLA

You meet (you meet) your Prince, (your Prince)
A charming (a charming) Prince,
As charming as a Prince will ever be!

CHARLOTTE & GABRIELLE

La, la, la, la, la
La, la, la, la

CHARLOTTE, GABRIELLE, MADAME, ELLA

The stars in a hazy heaven
Tremble above you
While he is whispering,

MADAME
(*As the* PRINCE)

"Darling, I love you!"

CHARLOTTE, GABRIELLE, MADAME, ELLA

You say goodbye,
Away you fly,

GABRIELLE & ELLA

But on your lips you keep a kiss,

MADAME & CHARLOTTE

All your life you'll dream of this

CHARLOTTE, GABRIELLE, MADAME, ELLA

Lovely, lovely night.
(CHARLOTTE, GABRIELLE, MADAME, *and* ELLA *dance.*)

CHARLOTTE, GABRIELLE, MADAME, ELLA

The stars in a hazy heaven
Tremble above you,
While he is whispering,

GABRIELLE

(*As the* PRINCE)

"Darling, I love you!"

CHARLOTTE, GABRIELLE, MADAME, ELLA

You say goodbye,
Away you fly,
But on your lips you keep a kiss,
All your life you'll dream of this,
Lovely, lovely, lovely,
Lovely night!

(*All four* WOMEN *sigh audibly.* MADAME *kisses* ELLA *on the head, quickly recoiling realizing what she has done.*)

MADAME

(*To* ELLA)

Isn't it wonderful how the needy just keep on going? Get up. Put away the—ah, whatever you call it.

(*To her* DAUGHTERS)

The only thing I have to comfort me after this disastrous evening is that the Prince seemed so completely devastated when his dream date ran away.

(ELLA *puts away the pianoforte.*)

CHARLOTTE

Oh, it was hilarious! The powder room was full of yammering when we were leaving. Why did the girl run away? My feeling is that up close the girl was physically unappealing.

MADAME

To bed, my lovely daughters. Cinderella, you stay here and clean up this pigsty of a parlor. Why is there a pumpkin on the table? It makes no design sense.

(MADAME *and* CHARLOTTE *exit.*)

GABRIELLE

Is there anything else you would like to know, Ella?

ELLA

No, it sounds like a really marvelous ball. I only wish I could have been there.

GABRIELLE

How did you know all that happened at the ball earlier this evening?

ELLA

I just . . . supposed it. Imagined it. Had a vision.

GABRIELLE

Interesting. (*Thrusts her right hand behind her own back*) Quick, how many fingers?

ELLA

Two?

GABRIELLE

Three. Fascinating. Where're your visions now?

ELLA

You're being silly. You're just picking on me just because I said the
Prince was wearing a white jacket and—

GABRIELLE

You didn't say it and he was. Something's going on here.

ELLA

You're being absurd. More than usual. I need to finish up and . . .
(ELLA *takes a kettle from the fire.*)

GABRIELLE

Let me help you with that.
(GABRIELLE *grabs* ELLA's *hand*)
Your hand is so callused and rough from work. Just like the hand
of the woman I shook this evening. Who danced with the prince.
(ELLA *pulls her hand back.*)

ELLA

I don't know what you're—

GABRIELLE

It was you tonight. Wasn't it?

ELLA

I—

GABRIELLE

It was you! How did you dance in glass shoes?
(ELLA *gasps, and runs out the door.* GABRIELLE *is right behind
her. The interior of the cottage transforms back into the exterior
yard.*)

ELLA

You won't tell the others, will you? Madame and Charlotte?

GABRIELLE

No. Never.

ELLA

Are you mad at me that I stole the Prince from you?

GABRIELLE

I will confess a secret to you. I never loved the Prince. Or even liked him. There's someone else that I want.

ELLA

How wonderful for you. Who is it?

GABRIELLE

Well, Madame hates him.

ELLA

Madame hating them doesn't narrow the field. Who is it?

GABRIELLE

If I promise to keep your secret of the Prince, can you keep my secret of my forbidden love?

ELLA

I can. And I will.

GABRIELLE

It's Jean-Michel. The firebrand.

ELLA

He is a good man. And seems angry for all the right reasons.

GABRIELLE

He wants to change the world and make it a better place. You gotta love a guy like that.

ELLA

You may one day win Jean-Michel. But I will never win Prince Topher. If he saw who I truly was, he would have no interest in me.

GABRIELLE

That's not true. He would love you for who you are.

ELLA

I don't see how.

GABRIELLE

Well, if Madame ever saw me with Jean-Michel, why I shudder to think what she might do! Are you sure you can keep my secret?

ELLA

I can. And you can keep mine. We shall have a secret. That will make us—

GABRIELLE

Co-conspirators.

ELLA

Friends.

GABRIELLE

Sisters.

> (ELLA *and* GABRIELLE *hug. They look at each other and smile.*
> *They have bonded.*)

ELLA

May we both find our loves.

GABRIELLE

And our lives.
> (*Sings*)
> The stars in a hazy heaven
> Trembling above me,

ELLA

Danced when he promised
Always to love me.

GABRIELLE

The day came through,

ELLA

Away I flew,
But on my lips he left a kiss—

GABRIELLE

All my life I'll dream of this

ELLA

Lovely—

GABRIELLE

Lovely—

ELLA

Lovely night.

(GABRIELLE *goes into the house.* ELLA *wanders into the forest. The scene transitions.*)

Scene Four

SCENE: *Another Part of the Forest*
(*Several days later. The full moon has become a crescent moon.
In another part of the forest,* TOPHER *enters, searching. He looks
at the moon in frustration.*)

TOPHER

I wake in the loneliness of sunrise
When the deep purple heaven turns blue,
And start to pray,
As I pray each day,
That I'll hear some word from you.
I lie in the loneliness of evening,
Looking out on a silver-flaked sea,
And ask the moon:
Oh, how soon, how soon
Will my love come home to me?
(ELLA *wanders forward. She and* TOPHER *don't see one another*)
I have found her

ELLA

I have found my angel

TOPHER

She's my angel

TOPHER & ELLA

With the dust of the stars in your eyes
We are dancing, we are flying
And she's/he's taking me back to the skies—
(ELLA *wanders offstage.*)

TOPHER

I lie in the loneliness of evening,
Looking out on a silver-flaked sea,
And ask the moon:
Oh, how soon, how soon
Will my love come home to me?
Will my love come home to me?
(*From the shadows comes* SEBASTIAN, *clutching a stack of papers.*)

SEBASTIAN

Honestly, sire. Three nights in a row you search? And here it is, four o'clock in the morning. It's as if you are testing my good nature. The second that woman in white ran off—which we all must admit seems to imply she has a police record. The second she is gone, you don't want to dance with any of the other girls.

TOPHER

Sebastian. Are there poor people in this kingdom who have had their land taken from them?

SEBASTIAN

If there were I would tell you.

TOPHER

Do they need our help?

SEBASTIAN

Everyone donated joyfully. Ignore this talk. Where did you hear it?

TOPHER

The girl.

SEBASTIAN

I don't know that she is to be trusted. Please come back to the castle, the work is piling up.

TOPHER

No, something isn't right.

SEBASTIAN

As you say— (*Puts his hand out*) The ring, sire.

TOPHER

Oh right, sorry. What are you stamping this time?

SEBASTIAN

Nothing, sire, hardly worth troubling your beautiful mind.

TOPHER

Let me read it.

SEBASTIAN

I should explain, before—

TOPHER

I'll read this—on my own.

SEBASTIAN

Your Future Majesty, let's go back to the palace and allow me to draw up some coverage you don't want to—

TOPHER

I'm reading this now. Thank you.

                    SEBASTIAN
But—

                    TOPHER
That will be all Sebastian. I'll ask you if I need anything explained.
    (SEBASTIAN *hands over the papers.* TOPHER *reads a bit. He sees*
    something shocking)
Oh . . . no.
    (*Reads more. Then stops*)
Sebastian!!

                    SEBASTIAN
Sire, I can explain—

                    TOPHER
How could you do this in my name?

                    SEBASTIAN
I am maintaining this life for you, without my watchful eye you
should be a pauper, would you like that?

                    TOPHER
I want that girl, the one who talked to me. I want to talk to that
girl.

                    SEBASTIAN
A troublemaker.

                    TOPHER
We're having another ball, a banquet. And she'll come to that!

SEBASTIAN

She won't show, this is lunacy!!

TOPHER

She will come! We're having a banquet tonight. And you are inviting everyone in the kingdom.

SEBASTIAN

Don't forget who you're talking to.

TOPHER

And don't you forget who you're talking to. Now we are having a banquet tonight and I am finding that girl!

SEBASTIAN

Very well, sire.
(*Storms off. Then stops and turns*)
She won't come. You don't even know her name! And if she really thought you were worthy of all her high ideals, she would have stayed, wouldn't she?!

TOPHER

A banquet!!!

SEBASTIAN
(*To* LORD PINKLETON)
The Prince is looking dreamy-eyed—
He has since giving the ball
And still he wants to find his bride,
The one he lost at the ball.
(*Spoken*)
So spread the word through the land. The Prince is throwing a banquet.

LORD PINKLETON & HERALDS

Hear ye!
Hear ye!

SEBASTIAN

It is his wish that the woman he met at the ball will attend. As
for the rest of us, well, what can I say—there's gonna be a ham.
Talk it back to me!

LORD PINKLETON & HERALDS

Hear ye!
Hear ye!

SEBASTIAN

And of course—I want to keep an eye on what women are there!
I'm not giving up control this time! Spread the word!
        (*Exits.*)

LORD PINKLETON & HERALDS

Hear ye!
Hear ye!
        (MADAME *enters among the* HERALDS.)

LORD PINKLETON
        (*Ringing his bell*)

His Royal Highness
Christopher Rupert James
Is giving a . . .

LORD PINKLETON & HERALDS

Banquet! . . . Tonight!! Invitation only!

MADAME
(*Taking an invitation from* LORD PINKLETON)
A banquet!!! Tonight!!! Cinderella, where are you? Cinderella—
where can you be?

LORD PINKLETON
(*Ringing his bell*)
His Royal Highness
Christopher Rupert,
Dopey and dream-eyed,
Can't find his lady—
Hoping to see her—
Asking where is she—

MADAME
Cinderella!! Where is she?

LORD PINKLETON & HERALDS
—Gregory James
Is giving . . .
(*The scene has transitioned to the interior of* MADAME'*s cottage.*)

Scene Five

SCENE: *Inside Madame's Cottage*
(GABRIELLE *sits at the table with an invitation.* MADAME *enters through the door.*)

MADAME

A banquet! Why does the Prince do this? It seems cruelty beyond measure! Two significant social events in one week. Now granted I have never looked lovelier. But my physical perfection comes at a price.
(*Looks at her hands*)
Gloves, that's what it was! Cinderella! Where are the gloves?
(MADAME *runs off into the backroom, just as* ELLA *enters the house.*)

GABRIELLE

Ella, over here. Don't tell her you have the gloves quite yet, yes I know, she'll be abusive later, but trust me, this shall be worth it! I am going to tell Madame that I am sick—

ELLA

Would you like some—

GABRIELLE

I'm not really sick, I'm pretending! It's just like when Charlotte was in school and pretended to be sick to get out of things she didn't like, like the third and fourth grades. I will be sick just as we are leaving for the carriage. Madame and Charlotte will leave without me. I will then change back into my regular clothes and meet my secret crush Jean-Michel—I'm taking him up on his offer to go help in a soup kitchen!

ELLA

A soup kitchen?

GABRIELLE

I get to ladle! You heard me. And guess what will happen to this beautiful dress and invitation? I shall loan them both to you—you shall go in my stead! And meet the Prince and fall in love and get married and exact revenge on Madame and try to keep Jean-Michel out of the stockade. Tra-la-tra-la, the way my mind works.

MADAME
(*Offstage*)

Cinderella! I can't find my gloves!

GABRIELLE

And don't worry about Madame, she never notices anything that isn't her.

ELLA

Your gloves are right here, Madame!

MADAME
(*Entering*)

Why did you not tell me you had the gloves, foolish child? Charlotte!! Make haste, child! And those shoes are delicate and dainty.

CHARLOTTE
(*Hobbling*)

My feet burn with the heat of a hundred suns!

MADAME

To the carriage, daughters.

GABRIELLE
(*Grabbing her abdomen, and letting out a yelp*)
Oooooh! Madame—my stomach, I must have eaten something
this morning that disagrees with me.
(*Sits.*)

MADAME
No, no—this can't prevent me from going to the banquet tonight.

GABRIELLE
Go—you go without me—let Charlotte meet the Prince and
steal him from the homely girl from the ball—Go—let Charlotte
become queen!

CHARLOTTE
I think I can make that work.

MADAME
I shall do this battle with only half my troops. Cinderella, fetch
the physician. If Gabrielle is better, send her to the castle imme-
diately. Gabrielle, get better. I insist on it. Keep your invitation.

GABRIELLE
Thank you, Mother. I'll come if I feel bette—
(*Makes a vomit sound.*)

MADAME
Not on the dress! Charlotte, the carriage awaits.
(MADAME *and* CHARLOTTE *sweep out.* ELLA *is about to say
something.*)

GABRIELLE

Sshhh.

(*The sound of the carriage leaving.* GABRIELLE *runs into the back room*)

Quickly, I'll change and you—you knock on the door.

(ELLA *does so. It knocks back.*)

ELLA

It knocked back.

GABRIELLE
(*Offstage*)

Then open it.

(ELLA *opens the door.* JEAN-MICHEL *enters.*)

JEAN-MICHEL

Hello, Ella!

ELLA

Well, hello, Jean-Michel.

JEAN-MICHEL

I am sick of hiding in the shadows like a fearful person.

ELLA

Would you rather see Madame?

JEAN-MICHEL

Hiding is nice.

ELLA

How are you this evening?

JEAN-MICHEL

I'm going out with Gabrielle and I'm wound up like a tick. To-night, she and I will go to the green grocer and beg him for whatever scraps he might have, then we shall slave over a hot stove and serve a meal to the very poorest. I do hope she's not expecting that much fun every night.

GABRIELLE
(*Entering in a simple dress*)
Good evening, Jean-Michel.

JEAN-MICHEL
Good evening, Gabrielle. I much prefer you in this simple attire. You no longer look like a carnival attraction.

GABRIELLE
You speak such kind words to me, all the day long. And what of the soup kitchen this evening?
(ELLA *exits.*)

JEAN-MICHEL
Our first responsibility is with the poor. Then we shall march to the palace steps and I shall speak with the Prince. We only have one thing to worry about.

GABRIELLE
What's that?

JEAN-MICHEL
That he'll even speak to me.

GABRIELLE

Well, Ella might be a help, you know she's talked to the Prince.

JEAN-MICHEL

What?! Ella talked to the Prince?!

GABRIELLE

She went to the ball! They were talking about the kingdom and how to make things better. And tonight, she is going to the banquet!

JEAN-MICHEL

The world is upside down!! But don't you know what this means? If she really talked to the Prince, then I can talk to him and he'll be open to my suggestions. What do you call this feeling I have?

GABRIELLE

Optimism.

JEAN-MICHEL

Optimism. I have to do this more often.

GABRIELLE

(*Grabbing a bottle of wine and two glasses*)
You can march up to the Prince and talk to him.

JEAN-MICHEL

I can march up to the Prince and talk to him.

GABRIELLE

You can be a leader!

JEAN-MICHEL

I can be a leader!

GABRIELLE

You can be my boyfriend!

JEAN-MICHEL

I can be your boyfriend. Whoa, left turn! What are you doing?
This looks very counter-revolutionary.

GABRIELLE

I like the man who wants to change the world, but I also like the
man who brought me flowers.

JEAN-MICHEL

Who brought you flowers? Oh, I did. No, I couldn't.

GABRIELLE

You just said so. Optimism.

JEAN-MICHEL

Optimism?

GABRIELLE
(*Handing glass*)

Let yourself go.

JEAN-MICHEL
(*Drinks wine*)

I could be your boyfriend?

GABRIELLE

Yes!

JEAN-MICHEL

Yes! Yes! (*Kisses her*) Am I your boyfriend?

GABRIELLE

Yes!

JEAN-MICHEL

Yes!!!

(JEAN-MICHEL *and* GABRIELLE *kiss passionately.* MADAME *walks in.*)

MADAME

So that's how it is?

(JEAN-MICHEL *and* GABRIELLE *quickly pull apart and gasp at the sight of* MADAME.)

GABRIELLE

Mama!

MADAME

My own daughter—my flesh and blood deceiving me with someone so decidedly unsuitable. I had plans for you, Gabrielle, I had created a life for you and this is how you show your gratitude—

(ELLA *enters in* GABRIELLE'*s dress, holding her invitation.*)

ELLA

All dressed up and ready for court. How do I look?

MADAME

And you! Do you think you could go to court? I never loved
your father. I just wanted his money. You've been nothing but a
nuisance to me since the day he died. You think you can wear a
beautiful gown? You think that is acceptable? You should be in
rags.
(MADAME *rips* ELLA's *dress.*)

MADAME

Worn-out rags, that's all you deserve.
(MADAME *shreds the dress.*)

ELLA

No!

GABRIELLE

Mother, please stop!

MADAME

I am no longer your mother. You! Gabrielle, get out of my house,
you are no longer welcome here—to the devil with you!
(MADAME *throws the bits of torn dress at* GABRIELLE *and* JEAN-
MICHEL *as they turn and run off.* MADAME *picks up the invitation and tears it up, turning to the now sobbing* ELLA.)

MADAME

I'll decide what to do with you later. (*Begins to storm off, then stops*)
Why did you have to make me doubt myself, I was doing so well?
(*Exits.*)
(ELLA *cries. The sack of rags is there. Then some smoke begins to
trail out from the china cabinet. And light comes from within.
The smoke then grows and grows and opens, revealing* MARIE,
in her beautiful gown. She enters.)

ELLA

At last, a friendly face.

MARIE

Ella, sweet child, hurry, you shall be late for the banquet.

ELLA

No, look, everything is ruined.

MARIE

Hurry. The Prince needs you. He wants you.

ELLA

No, I can't—

MARIE

Why do you think he's having this second event tonight? To try to find you.

ELLA

Every time I take a step forward Madame pushes me back. The Prince would never love me if he saw me as I truly am. I can't keep fighting.

MARIE

If you have a dream, then very soon thereafter you're going to have to fight for it. Why, otherwise, how would you know the dream is yours?

ELLA

But my life—

MARIE

Exactly. It is your life.

MARIE
(*Sings*)
Beyond the voice that keeps insisting "no,"
There is something more than doubting
Breaking through the darkness.
Something that sets your heart aglow.

Someone wants you,
You know who.
Now you're living—
There's music in you.

Now you're hearing
Something new,
Someone playing
The music in you.

Now you're living,
You know why,
Now there's nothing
You won't try—

Move a mountain,
Light the sky,
Make a wish come true—
There is music in you.

ELLA

But I can't go to the banquet. My clothing is in tatters. It's all I
have.

MARIE

Yes, perhaps we need even more tatters. More rags, rags, rags!

ELLA

But—

MARIE

Rags, rags, rags!!!
(*Spoken rhythmically*)
Tatters and shatters in bags
Make the new from old.
Tatters that matter and rags
Spin them into gold!
(ELLA *throws the rags into the air. As they land, her torn gown has transformed into something golden and stunning.* ELLA *is amazed.*)

MARIE

Now place these rags in your bag. Now remember the magic is gone at midnight!
(ELLA *gathers up the rags on the floor.*)

ELLA

Yes, the magic is gone at midnight. Is there anything else?

MARIE

Well, the glass slippers are already upon your feet and—oh yes! This book, that Jean-Michel gave you about the world. Now you only have the entire world to help you!
(*The cottage transforms into exterior woods.*)

MARIE

Now you can go
Wherever you want to go.
Now you can do
Whatever you want to do.

Now you can be
Whatever you want to be,
And love is the song
You will sing your whole life through.

Move a mountain,
Light the sky,
Make a wish come true—
There is music in you.
(MARIE *and* ELLA *exit.*)

Scene Six

SCENE: *The Palace Steps*
(*The banquet* GUESTS, *including* CHARLOTTE *and* MADAME, *arrive and greet* LORD PINKLETON *and* SEBASTIAN. *They make a fuss over* TOPHER, *who examines every* WOMAN'*s face and then seems distracted.*)

LORD PINKLETON

Dinner is served!
(*The* GUESTS *run up the stairs excitedly.* CHARLOTTE *is the last. Stopping halfway up the stairs, she turns to* TOPHER.)

CHARLOTTE
(*Pointing to self*)
This is still an option.
(TOPHER *and* SEBASTIAN *alone.*)

SEBASTIAN

You Majestic Highness, I believe all the guests have arrived. It's time for the banquet.

TOPHER

I'm waiting for her. She has to come.

SEBASTIAN

Very well, sire, but be warned this party is a pack of gossips. I'd hurry it along if I were you.
(SEBASTIAN *goes into the palace. A moment, then* TOPHER *turns to go up the stairs.* ELLA *runs on in her gold dress, holding the book.*)

ELLA

Prince Topher!

TOPHER

You're here!

ELLA

I'm sorry I'm late, I'm so glad—

TOPHER

I knew if I had a banquet you would come!

ELLA

And I'm sorry I ran away before—

TOPHER

And you're even more beautiful than I remembered.

ELLA

Did you really have this banquet just for me?

TOPHER

I would have a hundred banquets to find you.

ELLA

Really? And the thing about me being more beautiful than you remember, that's real, too?

TOPHER

Yes, yes, of course.

ELLA

Wow. What do you know about that?

TOPHER

I've been thinking about you. And I've been thinking of what you were saying about the people having their homes taken away. The court tells me I should just ignore such talk but—

ELLA

But, you know that if you're going to be king, you have to pay attention to things that people tell you to ignore.

TOPHER

Yes, yes. I want to meet all of my people, not only the ones that Sebastian lets me see. I just don't know how, it's impossible.

ELLA

Oh, that's going to be more possible than you can even imagine. My friend Jean-Michel and my sister Gabrielle are headed here right now with some of your people.

TOPHER

Talk to me? But—if things are as bad as you say they are then they'll be angry with me.

ELLA

I think if you can do battle with a giant or a dragon, you can handle a person who just wants to talk to you.

TOPHER

Okay, you're good.

ELLA

Just be yourself. They'll see the man that I see—
(*The sound of the* GROUP *approaching.*)

TOPHER

Wait, what's your name?

ELLA

Just trust me, because I am your one true friend.
(*The* CROWD, *led by* JEAN-MICHEL *and* GABRIELLE, *enters.*)

ELLA

Friends, come meet Prince Topher. (*To* GABRIELLE *and* JEAN-MICHEL) Just don't say my name.

GABRIELLE

I won't say your name. I won't even ask about the gold dress.

JEAN-MICHEL

Are you all right?

ELLA

Yes. Yes. (*To* TOPHER) Jean-Michel is a wonderful man with a lot of great ideas.

JEAN-MICHEL
(*Beginning to bow*)

I—

TOPHER

No, no. It's nice to meet you.
(TOPHER *and* JEAN-MICHEL *shake hands.*)

ELLA

And Gabrielle, my sister.
> (TOPHER *and* GABRIELLE *shake hands.* ELLA *approaches*
> YVONNE *with a baby and* SAM.)

ELLA

And this is Yvonne and her baby.

TOPHER

I see the resemblance.

ELLA

This is Sam.

SAM

It is an honor to meet you.

TOPHER
> (*Shaking* SAM's *hand*)

It is an honor to meet you.
> (*The* PEASANTS *surround* TOPHER.)

SAM

Hey, this prince is all right.
> (YVONNE *puts her baby in* TOPHER's *arms.*)

TOPHER

Okay, I'm holding a baby.

SAM

You can talk to him like a person!
> (YVONNE *takes the baby from* TOPHER.)

ELLA

Prince Topher, Jean-Michel has something he'd like to say to you.

JEAN-MICHEL

I—uh—we—these people have had their homes and property taken from them. I've said this before, but now I know what it is to have someone you love lose their home. We need your help. We need to have our voices heard.
(*Sings*)
For you can't just wait to be served by fate
On a silver plate or a tray.

JEAN-MICHEL & GABRIELLE

Now is the time,
The time of your life,
The time of your life is today.

TOPHER

Yes, yes, I see and true me, I too know what it's like to be overlooked. I want to help you but how?

MARIE
(*Offstage*)

Fol-de-rol and fiddledy dee,
Fiddledy faddlely fumble,
All the dreams in all the world
Go "oops" and out they tumble!
(*The book falls from* ELLA's *hands.*)

ELLA

Of course. It's here.

TOPHER

What's here?

ELLA
(*Shows book to* TOPHER)

Do you know it?

TOPHER

I read it at university.

ELLA
(*Opening the book*)

Look, chapter two.

TOPHER
(*Looking over* ELLA'*s shoulder*)

Of course, chapter two!

JEAN-MICHEL
(*Looking over* ELLA'*s shoulder*)

Chapter two! I didn't get that far.

TOPHER
(*Taking the book*)

Yes, yes. Chapter two. I should have known! People, I think I
have a plan.

ELLA

I knew you would.

SAM

Long live Prince Topher.
(*A cheer from the* CROWD.)

CLAUD

Our future king!
(*A loud cheer from the* CROWD. SEBASTIAN, LORD PINKLETON,
MADAME, CHARLOTTE, *and the other* MEMBERS OF THE COURT,
rush on. ELLA *quickly hides under the stairs.*)

SEBASTIAN

Prince Topher, what are you doing surrounded by these ragamuffins?

TOPHER

Sebastian, you said no one needed my help—what do you call
these people?

SEBASTIAN

From their attire, I assume artists.

JEAN-MICHEL

We demand to have our voices heard.
(*A cheer from the* CROWD.)

SEBASTIAN

A beheading would not be out of place here.

TOPHER

Yes, all the people must be heard. That's a very good idea.

SEBASTIAN

What is going on?

TOPHER

Now there is a way for all to be seen and heard. It's in this book.
In one month, let's all vote for a new job I shall create, the post

of . . . Prime Minister. Someone who will counsel me. I nominate
our current Lord Protector, Sebastian.

SEBASTIAN

I am unworthy, sire.

TOPHER

And I also nominate this man, Jean-Michel.

SEBASTIAN & MADAME
(*Almost overlapping*)

What?!

TOPHER

Let the people decide. The way things are or the way things could
be. And everyone, rich or poor, only gets one vote.

SEBASTIAN

One person, one vote? Where's the fun in that?

TOPHER

People, in one month, I give you—an election!!!

CROWD

What a guy! What a guy!
He's a plain and simple,
Complicated, fascinating—
  (TOPHER *is about to turn and leave, when he sees* ELLA, *from
  the back of the* CROWD. *She mimes eating, trying to give*
  TOPHER *a clue.*)

TOPHER

Oh, right. Good idea. And now everyone, rich and poor, into the castle for a free banquet!

(*Cheers from the* PEASANTS—*and terror from the* COURT—*as* ALL *run into the castle. Only* ELLA *and* TOPHER *are left.*)

ELLA

You did it!! I knew you could!

TOPHER

I did do it! And I think I know who I am now!

ELLA

You're smiling. I've seen you smile before, but never like that.

TOPHER

I know the king that I can be. Just, fair. Kind-hearted. I've found myself and you showed me the way.

ELLA

You seem so sure of yourself. So sure of everything.

TOPHER

I feel like I can answer any question that gets thrown at me!

ELLA

You can!

TOPHER

With you I can. There's only one question I don't have an answer for.

Do I love you

Because you're beautiful?
Or are you beautiful
Because I love you?
Am I making believe I see in you
A girl too lovely to
Be really true?
Do I want you
Because you're wonderful?
Or are you wonderful
Because I want you?
Are you the sweet invention of a lover's dream,
Or are you really as beautiful as you seem?

ELLA

Am I making believe I see in you
A man too perfect to
Be really true?
Do I want you
Because you're wonderful?
Or are you wonderful
Because I want you?

ELLA & TOPHER

Are you the sweet invention of a lover's dream,
Or are you really as beautiful as you seem?
  (ELLA *and* TOPHER *kiss.*)

TOPHER

And now I feel we can really change the world. You and I.

ELLA

To the banquet?

TOPHER

To the banquet!

ELLA

What time is it?

TOPHER

Only midnight, why?

ELLA

Midnight! I have to go!

TOPHER

Again? Why?

ELLA

I— (*The clock continues to strike midnight*) I must go

TOPHER

How can you leave me? Why do you leave?

ELLA

If you knew who I really was, you'd never want me.

TOPHER

Don't leave me!

ELLA

I don't want to, but I have to.

TOPHER

Wait! Guards, anyone, help! (*She runs off. He chases her*) Stop!!

Someone stop her!!

> (ELLA *runs down the stairway, then stops and looks up at* TOPHER. ELLA *takes off her glass slipper and places it on the staircase.* TOPHER *picks up the slipper and looks at it*)

Ha!

Scene Seven

SCENE: *The Palace*
(LORD PINKLETON *rings his bell, and makes his announcement.*)

LORD PINKLETON

Hear ye!
(*Rings bell*)
Hear ye!
(*Rings bell*)
Eight o'clock and all is well. A great day in the kingdom. In one month will be our first free election for Prime Minister of the land. The candidates are Jean-Michel and our current Lord Protector, Sebastian. But tomorrow, all women, come to the palace and try on the glass slipper. Whosoever fits it shall be married to the Prince! This is the biggest news cycle I have ever shouted. I'll be back at eleven with local weather and sports.
(*Sings*)
Hear ye!
(*Rings bell*)
Hear ye!
(*Rings bell*)
The prince intends
To search until
He finds the girl
Who fits the bill.
Well, not "the bill,"
The shoe I mean,
A shoe to fit a queen!

    (*As* LORD PINKLETON *sings, a line of* WOMEN *forms, waiting to try on the slipper.* TOPHER *kneels by a chair, holding the slipper. An* OFFICIAL *looks on.* LORD PINKLETON *presides over the shoe-fitting, giving the official decree.*)

LORD PINKLETON
(TOPHER *tries the slipper on a* WOMAN)
The shoe does not fit!
(TOPHER *tries the slipper on another* WOMAN)
The shoe does not fit!

TOPHER
We're going to find that girl. If the shoe is made of glass it could only fit one person. I mean that's why she left it, right?

LORD PINKLETON
It doesn't look good.
(TOPHER *tries the slipper on yet another* WOMAN. *The other* WOMEN *push against her, attempting to get her foot into the shoe.*)

SEBASTIAN
(*Entering*)
How goes it?

OFFICIAL
So far, no luck.
(TOPHER *tries the slipper on two more* WOMEN. MADAME *and* CHARLOTTE *enter.*)

MADAME
Now, when you try on the shoe, make eye contact with His Highness. For our family, you shall try the shoe on first.

CHARLOTTE

Don't you mean only? No one has seen Cinderella since you yelled at her two nights ago. You got rid of Gabrielle because she likes that guy who might be our new Prime Minister—wow—good call there!

MADAME

I don't know what is going on in this world. Everything I felt was holy and true is trash. That which meant nothing to me now appears to mean everything.

CHARLOTTE

Here goes nothin'. (*To* TOPHER) Me again. Hey. (*Tries on the slipper*)
          (GABRIELLE *and* JEAN-MICHEL *enter from opposite sides of the stage.*)

JEAN-MICHEL

Gabrielle, there you are! I've just decided, if I become Prime Minister, I'm gonna marry you!

GABRIELLE

Wow, the stakes are really piling up!

LORD PINKLETON
          (*The slipper does not fit* CHARLOTTE'*s foot*)
It does not fit.

CHARLOTTE

Of course it doesn't fit. I'm not the girl the Prince has fallen in love with. None of us are that girl.

TOPHER

Is that the last eligible lady in the kingdom?

LORD PINKLETON

She appears to be, yes.

TOPHER

She can't be!

SEBASTIAN

I told you the girl wouldn't come. Can we end this charade?

TOPHER

Everyone truly tried on the slipper?
   (*The* CROWD *shouts and mumbles.* ELLA *has entered behind them.*)

ELLA

I haven't tried on the slipper.
   (*The* CROWD *parts, revealing* ELLA, *in her provincial garb, just as it did earlier at the ball.* MARIE, *in her rags, is with her.*)

MARIE

Everything has led you to this moment. Now you have something to believe in: yourself.
   (*Sings*)
   All the dreamers in the world
   Are dizzy in the noodle.
      (MARIE *disappears into the* CROWD. ELLA *approaches the chair.*)

MADAME

By all means, make yourself ridiculous, try on the slipper.

SEBASTIAN

It's too, too rich!

JEAN-MICHEL

You can do it.

GABRIELLE

That's my sister!
(ELLA *reaches* TOPHER *at the chair.*)

TOPHER

Have we met before?

ELLA

Yes, and we are seeing each other for the first time right now.
(TOPHER *tries the slipper on* ELLA. *It fits.* EVERYONE *gasps.*)

LORD PINKLETON
(*Amazed*)

The shoe fits!

TOPHER

It is you. You who danced with me, you who showed me my own
kingdom . . . and offered me water that day I was thirsty. Please
don't run away again, I don't think I could bear it.
(ELLA *nods.* EVERYONE *bows.*)

MADAME

It was . . . you? We both know how horribly I have treated you
since your father's death. I know it is beyond reason to expect
some of your famous kindness. I am not worthy.

ELLA

Madame, you have treated me very poorly indeed. And I say to you now the three kindest words I know. I forgive you.

MADAME

(*Bows in gratitude*)

Thank you.

CHARLOTTE

Do you think that includes me?

MADAME

For you it probably involves several hours of community service.

TOPHER

You're amazing, could . . . I maybe learn your name now?

ELLA

Cinderella.

TOPHER

Cinderella, it's beautiful.

ELLA

It's a name I once hated, but starting today, I'll keep. So that from now on, when anyone thinks something is impossible, they'll just say my name. And know better.

TOPHER

Cinderella, I love you so much, I don't know what to do.

ELLA

Oh. Well. Is marriage still on the table?

TOPHER

Yes. Yes. Oh, my—yes!! You have to marry me. I mean, will you marry me? Oh, wait. (*Gets down on one knee*) Cinderella, will you marry me?

ELLA

Yes, my handsome Prince. I will marry you.
(TOPHER *rises.*)

TOPHER & ELLA
(*In counterpoint harmony*)
In the arms of my love I'm flying
Over mountain and meadow and glen,

TOPHER

And I like it so well

ELLA

And I like it so well

TOPHER

That for all I can tell

ELLA

. . . I like it so well

TOPHER & ELLA

And I like it so well
That for all I can tell
I may never come down again!
I may never come down to earth again!

Scene Eight

SCENE: *The Royal Gardens*
(*The wedding ceremony of* ELLA *and* TOPHER. ALL *are dressed in white.* TRUMPETERS *enter.* LORD PINKLETON *enters, followed by* GUARDS *holding flower bouquets.*)

LORD PINKLETON & CHORUS
The fields are aglow in autumn yellow,
And the sky is a robin's egg blue.
It makes you wish,
When you fall asleep,
You will dream about the view.
(*The* WOMEN *of the* CHORUS *enter, throwing rose petals.*)
Bizarre and improbable and pretty
As a page from the fairy-tale books,
It makes you wish
That the world could be
As lovely as it looks.
(MADAME *and* SEBASTIAN *enter from one side of the stage, with* CHARLOTTE *behind them.* JEAN-MICHEL, *now dressed in the attire of a prime minister, enters with* GABRIELLE *by his side.* ALL *bow to* JEAN-MICHEL. SEBASTIAN *offers his hand to* JEAN-MICHEL. *They shake and ascend the steps of the palace.* MADAME *and* GABRIELLE *embrace in a hug.* CHARLOTTE *joins them. They follow up the steps.*)

CHORUS
All around you the same sweet sound
You can hear in the earth and down from the sky,
What a lucky girl,
What a lucky guy,

What a girl!
What a guy!
(MARIE *flies in.*)

MARIE & CHORUS
Someone wants you,
You know who.
Now you're living—
There's music in you.
(ELLA *enters in her wedding gown. The* RACCOON *and* FOX *are in a tree, holding a bouquet of flowers.* ELLA *takes the bouquet, and the* THREE *bow to one another.* TOPHER *descends the steps. He bows.* ELLA *curtsies. They ascend the steps.*)

MARIE & CHORUS
Now you can go
Wherever you want to go.
Now you can do
Whatever you want to do.

Now you can be
Whatever you want to be,
And love is the song
You will sing your whole life through.

FULL COMPANY
Move a mountain,
Light the sky,
Make a wish come true—
There is music—
(*The clock starts to chime midnight.* ALL *look to* ELLA.)

ELLA

I'm good.

(TOPHER *and* ELLA *kiss.*)

FULL COMPANY

—In you!

(TOPHER *and* ELLA *wave to their* SUBJECTS. *Curtain calls.*)

FULL COMPANY

But the world is full of zanies and fools
Who don't believe in sensible rules
And won't believe what sensible people say,
And because these daft and dewy-eyed dopes
Keep building up impossible hopes,
Impossible things are happ'ning every day!

(*The curtain falls. End of Act Two.*)

PHOTOGRAPH CREDITS